Breweries, Politics and Identity

Tycho van der Hoog

Breweries, Politics and Identity
The History Behind Namibian Beer

Basler Afrika Bibliographien 2019

©2019 The authors
©2019 The photographers
©2019 Basler Afrika Bibliographien

Basler Afrika Bibliographien
Namibia Resource Centre & Southern Africa Library
Klosterberg 23
4051 Basel
Switzerland
www.baslerafrika.ch

The Basler Afrika Bibliographien is part of the Carl Schlettwein Foundation

All rights reserved.

Cover photos: A group of influential settlers sitting outside a house and drinking beer, National Archives of Namibia, no. 01407 (above); The crew from the brewery at Omaruru, from the collection of Gunter von Schumann (below).

ISBN 978-3-906927-12-1

Contents

Foreword by Anne Mager	vii
Acknowledgements	viii
Introduction	1
The Importance of Beer	3
The Research Project	7
Prelude: A Centuries-long Tradition of Home Brewing	9
1 The Advent of Formal Breweries, 1900–1920	14
The Arrival of European Settlers	14
How to Establish a Brewery	18
The Beer Triangle	22
The Great War	37
The Beer War	39
The Formation of South West Breweries	41
2 A Changing Beer Market, 1920–1970	44
Legal Consequences for Beer	44
Three New Breweries	47
Economic Depression	53
World War II	55
Problematic Liquor Law	59
The Change of the 1960s	67
3 Namibia Breweries' Transformation, 1970–2019	69
A South West Company	69
Challenge from South African Breweries	73
The North Opens Up	76
A New Direction	79
The Beer War is Back	91
The Long Road to a SAB Brewery	93

    An Ongoing Rivalry   95
    New Developments   98

Conclusion   100

Abbreviations   102

List of figures   103

Bibliography   104

Appendix 1: Overview of Breweries   113

Appendix 2: Traditional Brewing Recipes   116

Foreword

Not a beer drinker? No problem. *Breweries, Politics and Identity* looks through a warm amber-coloured lens to bring us a view not only of the beer industry but of a broad history of Namibia from the late 19th century to the present. To be sure, the establishment of breweries and the production of beer are in the centre of this view but there is much to be seen and enjoyed beyond the imperatives of a fermentation industry.

The book has great strengths. Tycho van der Hoog has collected a wonderful set of historical photographs that serve to illustrate the history of particular breweries, their staff and the changing nature of beer production. But these images also provide compelling vignettes of German settler society and the development of racial capitalism. We see how transport — central to the brewing industry — develops over time from a construction cart renovating Southwest Breweries during the Depression led by a team of donkeys in-spanned with a zebra to heavy articulated mine-proof Mercedes Benz trucks in the 1980s. Context is clearly drawn. These delivery cum military vehicles moved bottles of lager produced in Windhoek to the country's northern border with Angola during the liberation war.

Tycho also has a good ear and has gleaned fascinating tales of intrigue as breweries competed in the market place almost from the inception of the Namibian liquor industry. From the 1950s to the late 1990s, fierce battles between South West Breweries (later Namibian Breweries Ltd or NBL) and the South African Breweries (SAB) over brands and markets reached fever pitch in a series of beer wars.

In some ways, the Namibian story mirrors that of the brewing industry in South Africa, but Tycho has told a uniquely Namibian tale. Dozens of people have shared their memories and opened their family albums enabling him to bring out the local, the quirky and the nationalist elements of this history. The book is fun at the same time as it is serious and scholarly – a good read for everyone interested in southern Africa.

Anne Mager
Emeritus Professor at the Department of Historical Studies, University of Cape Town, and author of the book Beer, Sociability, and Masculinity in South Africa *(Indiana University Press, 2010).*

Acknowledgements

Beer might be considered as an odd subject for scholarship, but hopefully this book proves the opposite. Behind your favourite bottle of lager, ale or whatever your preferred drink might be, lies a complex world of powerful companies, intricate government legislation, and most importantly, history. It has been a privilege to spend a long time working on the brewing history of Namibia, a place that has left a profound influence on me. But sometimes it has also been a struggle. In any case, I owe my deepest thanks to Jan-Bart Gewald for his continuous guidance and advice. I am also indebted to Laura Mann for earlier comments on drafts of this book.

During my fieldwork in Namibia, I was lucky enough to meet the extraordinary librarians Armin Jagdhuber and Gunter von Schumann, both from the Namibia Scientific Society. I thoroughly enjoyed our conversations and I am grateful for the help you gave me during my research. I would also like to thank Nadine Kohlstädt and Trudi Stols for granting me access to the archives of the Scientific Society Swakopmund.

A highly rewarding aspect of my fieldwork was my interaction with Namibia Breweries Limited. Together with the good people from Snowballstudio, we developed a pop-up museum that dealt with Namibia's brewing history in 2016. I am grateful for the chance to talk to so many of NBL's employees, past and present, whose passion for brewing is unparalleled. In particular, I would like to thank Christin Obst, Christian Müller, Hans Herrmann and Stephan Koepp for their hospitality.

Most importantly, I would like to express my gratitude to all the people who have shared their stories with me, and in many cases also allowed me access to their collection of files, photos, beer bottles, beer labels, posters and other valuable artefacts that have greatly enriched the narrative of this book. In particular I would like to thank Lothar Geier and Harald Geier, Bernd Masche, Jeremy Silvester, Werner Hillebrecht, Mannfred Goldbeck, Brenda Bravenboer, Brigitte Schünemann, Don Stevenson, Bogart Butler, Linda Buckingham and Jörg Finkeldey. Anthy Schubert assisted me with German archival sources, thank you for your help.

Finally, I want to say a heartfelt thank you to the Basler Afrika Bibliographien, and in particular to Petra Kerckhoff and Sarah Schwarz, for the opportunity to publish this book.

Tycho van der Hoog
Leiden, December 2018

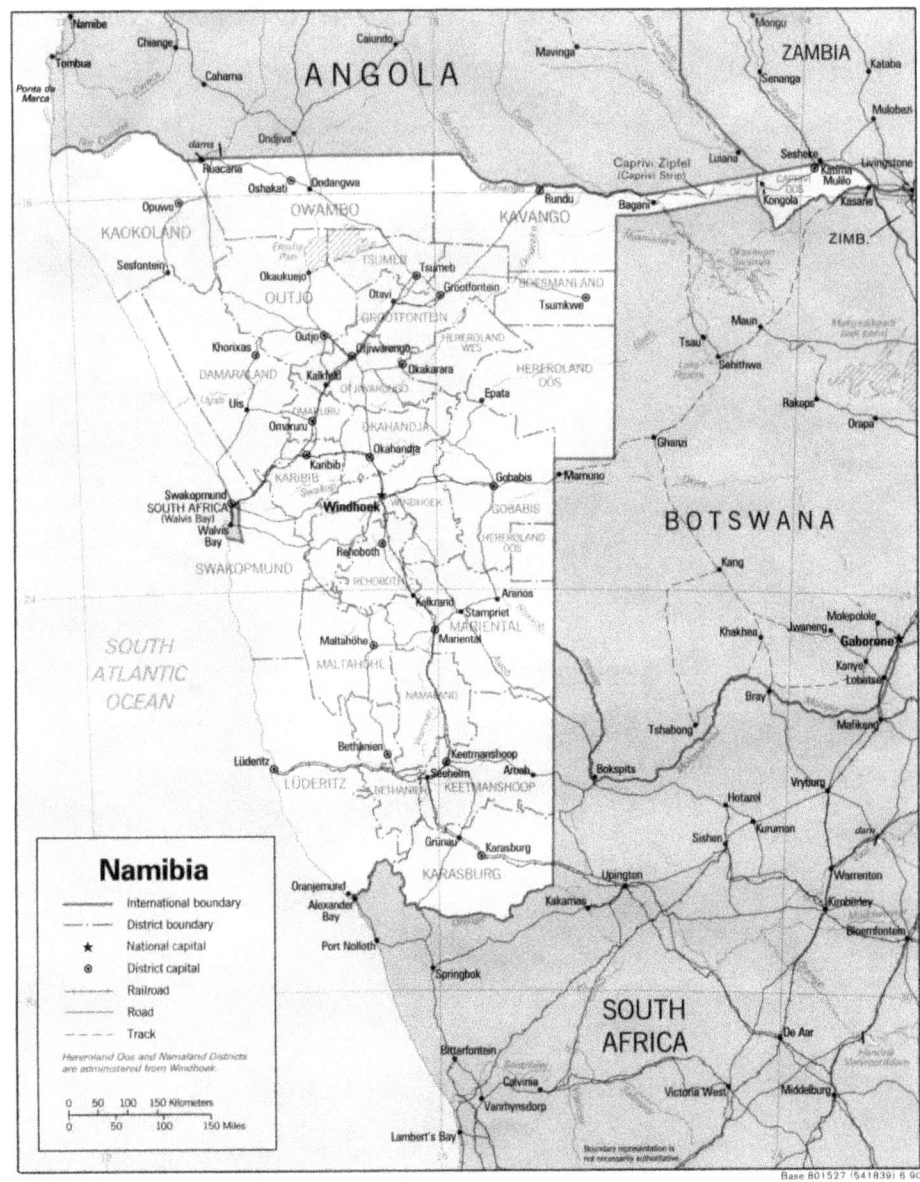

Fig. 1: Map of Namibia, 1990

This book is dedicated to Bo

Introduction

> You can't be a real country unless you have a beer and an airline. It helps if you have some kind of a football team, or some nuclear weapons, but at the very least you need a beer.
>
> Frank Zappa[1]

If Frank Zappa's playful comment — that a national beer is necessary for every 'real' country — is correct, then Namibia is on the right track. Namibian beer is available in around twenty countries all over the world, it continuously wins international awards for its quality and it is hugely popular in "the land of the brave," making Namibians proud. Since Namibia's independence in 1990, this alcoholic beverage has become one of the key characteristics of the Namibian nation. In the furthest corners of this enormous country one can find an ice-cold Windhoek Lager, Tafel Lager or another variant. The famous sundowner, where people watch the majestic sunsets while enjoying a cold beverage, has been developed into an art form.

However, for decades on end, this brew was not available to the black population as a consequence of apartheid politics, and the same beer actually emerged as a national icon for white settlers. It is a largely forgotten story with deep historical roots. This shows that the history of brewing in Namibia is far more than a simple story of beer: the beer market is an important political, economic and cultural factor that is intertwined with the general history of the country.

This book explains how European style beer was transformed from a settler's drink during colonial politics into a symbol of the independent Namibian nation. The beer market is a broad term for a variety of interacting actors: breweries, bottle stores and shebeens, consumers, the government, and liquor laws are examples. Hence, different angles are used to analyse this market. In this book, a historical perspective on the breweries is central. Breweries are conceptualised here as economic actors that have had to survive within a continuously changing socio-political context. Namibia's history is characterised by a succession of (colonial) administrations and beer became an increasingly politically loaded product. Today, however, the local brew is worldwide renowned as Namibian beer.

The reasons for studying the beer market in Namibia are threefold. Economically, beer constitutes a large economic market with a tremendous growth. Beer is a widely available

---

[1] F. Zappa with P. Occhiogrosso, 'America Drinks & Goes Marching', in: F. Zappa with P. Occhiogrosso, *The Real Frank Zappa Book* (New York 1999) 231.

and inexpensive commodity that penetrates all layers of society. Namibia Breweries Limited (NBL) is the largest private job provider and taxpayer of the country and is active in one of the largest national industries. Culturally, beer is a product with great significance. Beer and identity are closely related, which explains the many different brands aimed to target different groups of people. Beer also has severe implications on politics. Historically, liquor has been a way for governments to control the population and administrations are dependent on the tax revenues that are gained from beer consumption. Furthermore, Namibian beer makes the country worldwide renowned by exporting this product to almost twenty countries and getting global recognition in the form of awards. In terms of promoting the (touristic) image of Namibia, beer is an important instrument.

This book provides the first broad historical overview of the Namibian beer market, wherein the role of the breweries is highlighted. Over the past centuries, beer has played a central role in the everyday life of Namibians: it is a product with a profound history and many people thus have a personal connection to the beer industry. The structure of the book is straightforward. The remainder of the introduction will provide a short overview of previous studies on beer, showing that in the available literature more attention is given to South Africa than Namibia, although both countries share an intertwined liquor history. Hence, only a small body of publications deals with beer in Namibia, while the story of the breweries is seldom taken into account.

A prelude will highlight the centuries-long tradition of home brewing that still exists in Namibia to this day. It is important to note that beer is not a European invention, but already existed hundreds of years before the first foreign explorers set foot on Namibian soil. What follows is a broad historical narrative, divided into three chapters. The establishment of the first formal breweries in German South West Africa (GSWA) is discussed in Chapter One (spanning the time period of 1900–1920). A large number of small, scattered brewing companies sprung up after the German Protectorate was declared in 1884 and soon these breweries were in heavy competition with each other.

Chapter Two (spanning the time period 1920–1970) describes how the beer market radically changed within fifty years. This era started out with three breweries and two racially separated markets but ended with a single brewery that could cater to one, racially unified market. The remarkable transformation of NBL is the focus of Chapter Three (spanning the time period 1970–2015). This company had difficulties surviving as a small brewery that catered for "South Westers," the white settlers, but successfully adapted itself due to the threat of its competitor South African Breweries (SAB) and the opportunity that the Namibian independence of 1990 created. Finally, the Conclusion describes how commercial beer has shifted from a settler drink to a national symbol because of the close relations between the independent government and the brewery, and the threat of SAB, a foreign competitor from the country that once occupied Namibia.

The Importance of Beer

It may sound strange, but alcohol consumption has been researched for a long time.[2] The rich field of alcohol studies has a "chameleon character," in the words of scholar Deborah Bryceson: it offers a wide and colourful range of topics.[3] For this reason, the vast literature on this subject is difficult to summarise. Until the beginning of the 21st century, the study of alcohol has been primarily restricted to anthropologists.[4] Today, an eclectic range of scholars have researched alcohol in virtually all parts of Africa.[5]

Bryceson identified multiple facets of alcohol, which helps us to understand why it is important to see beer as more than 'just a drink.' According to her, alcohol has a strong religious and symbolic value. Rural ethnic areas often attach symbolic content to the production, distribution and consumption of traditional drinks. Urban-manufactured drinks are linked with ideas of modernity. Furthermore, alcohol has a social and psychological value. It is used to celebrate social occasions, drinking is a leisure activity and drinking spots are meeting places for people where they can exchange information. Alcohol also has economic and political value. Traditionally, fermented drinks provided basic food and drink, and alcohol is a medium for the exchange of opinions and ideas. Furthermore, the state traditionally has a strong interest in alcohol: taxation on liquor, for example, provides much-needed revenue for governments.[6]

---

[2] See e.g.; I. de Garine and V. de Garine (eds.), *Drinking: Anthropological Approaches* (New York 2001); M. Dietler, 'Alcohol: Anthropological/Archaeological Perspectives', *Annual Review of Anthropology* Vol. 35 (2006) 229–249; M. Douglas (ed.), *Constructive Drinking: Perspectives on Drink from Anthropology* (Cambridge 1987); H. Hahn, 'Consumption, Identities and Agency in Africa: Introduction', in: H. Hahn (ed.), *Consumption in Africa: Anthropological Approaches* (Berlin 2008) 9–42; D.G. Mandelbaum, 'Alcohol and Culture', *Current Anthropology* Vol 6. No. 3 (1965) 281–293.

[3] D. Bryceson (ed.), *Alcohol in Africa: Mixing Business, Pleasure, and Politics* (Portsmouth 2002) 3.

[4] Ibid., 3–4.

[5] Curto and Heap provided extensive lists with literature on studies on alcohol (in general). The last list was published more than twenty years ago but still contains relevant information. J.C. Curto, 'Alcohol in Africa: a preliminary compilation of the post-1875 literature', *A Current Bibliography on African Affairs*, Vol. 21 No. 1 (1989) 3–31; S. Heap, 'Alcohol in Africa: a supplementary list of post-1875 literature', *A Current Bibliography on African Affairs* Vol. 26 No. 1 (1994) 1–14. As an entry point on southern Africa, see J. Crush and C. Ambler (eds.), *Liquor and Labor in Southern Africa* (Athens 1992). J. Willis, *Potent Brews: A Social History of Alcohol in East Africa, 1850–1999* (Athens 2002) is a starting point for East Africa. For West Africa, E. Akyeampong, *Drink, Power and Cultural Change: A Social History of Alcohol in Ghana c. 1800 to Recent Times* (Portsmouth 1996) is a classic book.

[6] Bryceson (ed.), *Alcohol in Africa: Mixing Business, Pleasure, and Politics* (Portsmouth 2002) 5–9.

By far most works have been written on beer in South Africa.[7] The historical circumstances in South Africa (a combination of colonial interests in alcohol, the mining industry and urbanisation) resulted in heavy drinking cultures.[8] The main focus of most authors is placed on the impact of colonial alcohol legislation on the African population.[9] This is what Anne Mager calls the control-resistance model.[10] Less studied is the notion that South Africa severely influenced Namibia's beer market because it occupied South West Africa (SWA) for more than seventy years. Case in point is the fact that the liquor legislation of SWA was copied from the laws of South Africa. Only a small body of publications deals with beer in Namibia. Health studies have focused on the large problem of alcohol abuse in Namibia.[11] Some anthropological works have appeared on shebeens

---

[7] A. Mager, 'One Beer, "One Goal, One Nation, One Soul": South African Breweries, Heritage, Masculinity and Nationalism, 1960–1999', *Past and Present* Vol. 188 (2005) 163–194; A. Mager, 'White Liquor Hits Black Livers: Meanings of Excessive Liquor Consumption in South Africa in the Second Half of the Twentieth Century', *Social Science and Medicine* Vol. 59 (2004) 735–751; A. Mager, 'The First Decade of 'European Beer' in Apartheid South Africa: The State, the Brewers and the Drinking Public, 1962–72', *The Journal of African History* Vol. 40 No. 3 (1999) 367–388; A. Mager, *Beer, Sociability and Masculinity in South Africa* (Bloomington 2010); S.J. Britten, *One nation, one beer: The mythology of the new South Africa in advertising* (unpublished PhD thesis, 2006), University of Witwatersrand, Johannesburg; P. McAllister, *Xhosa Beer Drinking Rituals. Power, Practice and Performance in the South African Rural Periphery* (Durham 2006); P. McAllister, *Building the homestead: agriculture, labour and beer in South Africa's Transkei* (Leiden 2001); P. McAllister, 'Ubuntu and the Morality of Xhosa Beer Drinking: a Critical Appraisal' in: S. van Wolputte and M. Fumanti (eds.), *Beer in Africa: Drinking spaces, states and selves* (Münster 2010) 53–78 [not all works of McAllister are listed here, for more references for works on the same topic, see van Wolputte and Fumanti's edited volume, 294–295]; D. Whelan, 'The central beer hall as social and municipal infrastructure in twentieth century Pietermaritzburg', *Historia* Vol. 60 No. 1 (2015) 75–91; J.F.R. Lues, 'Brewing and consumptions practices of indigenous traditional beer in a typical South African semi-urban area', *Indilinga* Vol. 8 No. 2 (2009) 163–174; D. Atkinson, 'Contradictions of community within local government in the 1950s with reference to municipal beer trading', *New Contree* No. 57 (2009) 149–168; D. Atkinson, 'Complex negotiations in local governance: the municipal beer hall debate in East London, 1956 to 1962', *New Contree* No. 55 (2008) 93–113; R.M. Ralinala, 'Countering municipal monopoly in Mamelodi: an economic struggle, 1953, 1961', *South African Historical Journal* No. 46 (2002) 203–218; D. Krige, 'Inequality and Class through the Drinking Glass: An Ethnography of Men and Beer Consumption in Contemporary Soweto', in: S. van Wolputte and M. Fumanti (eds.), *Beer in Africa: Drinking spaces, states and selves* (Münster 2010) 223–256; E. Hellman, 'The Importance of Beer-Brewing in an Urban Native Yard' *Bantu Studies* Vol. 8 (1934) 39–60; P. la Hausse, 'Drink and Cultural Innovation in Durban: the Origins of the Beerhall in South Africa', in: J. Crush and C. Ambler, *Liquor and Labor in Southern Africa* (Athens 1992) 78–115; E. Rogerson, 'Drinking Apartheid and the Removal of Beerhalls in Johannesburg', in: J. Crush and C. Ambler (eds.), *Liquor and Labor in Southern Africa* (Athens 1992) 306–338.

[8] S. van Wolputte, and M. Fumanti (eds.), *Beer in Africa* 18, the authors paraphrase Bryceson: D. Bryceson (eds.), *Alcohol in Africa: Mixing Business, Pleasure, and Politics* (Portsmouth 2002) 277.

[9] R. Gordon, Inside the Windhoek Lager: Liquor and Lust in Namibia, in: W. Jankowiak and D. Bradburd (eds.) *Drugs, labor, and colonial expansion* (Tucson 2003) 122.

[10] A. Mager, 'The First Decade of 'European Beer' in Apartheid South Africa: The State, the Brewers and the Drinking Public, 1962–72', *The Journal of African History* Vol. 40 No. 3 (1999) 368.

[11] H. Siiskonen, 'Namibia and the Heritage of Colonial Alcohol Policy', *Nordic Journal of African Studies* Vol. 3 No. 1 (1994) 82; A. Pomuti and G. Eiseb, 'Alcohol abuse: a southern Namibian survey'

(small illicit bars, which are called cuca shops in northern Namibia) and *oshikundu* (a low alcoholic beverage).[12] Finally, a few historical studies dealt with the existence of colonial liquor laws during Namibia's turbulent history.[13]

The few studies on Namibian beer do show a strong connection between beer, politics and identity. Namibia's beer market does not solely consist of 'modern' beer (clear, industrially manufactured European-style lagers) but also has an important home brewing culture (often referred to as 'traditional'), as will be shown in the Prelude of this book. The production of modern beer increased tremendously over time. The government always had a far-reaching interest in drinking. Through liquor legislation, the state tried to regulate the beer market. For decades, the black population was not legally allowed to drink beer and the government tried to eradicate the inevitable illicit brewing of alcohol. Don Stevenson summarised this period of time with his statement that, historically, "the enjoyment of beer [...] is dependent upon your politics."[14]

Identity can be constructed through the consumption of beer. Researchers have stated that bars are places where Namibians can explore ideas on citizenship and the young

---

Windhoek: Namibian Institute for Social and Economic Research (1990); E. Lightfoot, M. Maree and J. Ananias, 'Exploring the relationship between HIV and alcohol use in a remote Namibian mining community', *African Journal of AIDS Research* Vol. 8, No. 3 (2009) 321–327; United Nations Development Programme, 'Alcohol and human development in Namibia, *Namibia human development report* (1999).

[12] S. van Wolputte, 'Beers and Bullets, Beads and Bulls. Drink and the Making of Margins in a Small Namibian Towns', in: S. van Wolputte and M. Fumanti (eds.), *Beer in Africa: Drinking Spaces, States and Selves* (Münster 2010) 79–105; M. Fumanti, '"I Like My Windhoek Lager": Beer Consumption and the Making of Men in Namibia', in: S. van Wolputte and M. Fumanti (eds.), *Beer in Africa: Drinking Spaces, States and Selves* (Münster 2010) 257–274; G. Dobler, 'License to Drink. Between Liberation and Inebriation in Northern Namibia', in: S. van Wolputte and M. Fumanti (eds.), *Beer in Africa: Drinking Spaces, States and Selves* (Münster 2010) 167–191; W. Embashu et al., 'Processing methods of Oshikundu, a traditional beverage from sub-tribes within Aawambo culture in the Northern Namibia', *Journal for Studies in Humanities and Social Sciences* Vol. 2, No. 1 (2013) 117–127. A selection of the authors dealt with the same topic in other publications, namely: W. Embashu, A. Cheikhyoussef, G. Kahaka, *Survey on Indigenous Knowledge and Household processing methods of Oshikundu; a cereal-based fermented beverage from Oshana, Oshikoto, Ohangwena and Omusati Regions in Namibia*, Multidisciplinary Research Centre, University of Namibia (Windhoek 2012).

[13] H. Siiskonen, 'Namibia and the Heritage of Colonial Alcohol Policy', *Nordic Journal of African Studies* Vol. 3 No. 1 (1994) 77–86; J.B. Gewald, 'Diluting Drinks and Deepening Discontent: Colonial Liquor Controls and Public Resistance in Windhoek, Namibia', in: D. Bryceson (ed.), *Alcohol in Africa: Mixing Business, Pleasure, and Politics* (Portsmouth 2002) 117–138; R. Gordon, Inside the Windhoek Lager: Liquor and Lust in Namibia, in: W. Jankowiak and D. Bradburd (eds.) *Drugs, labor, and colonial expansion* (Tucson 2003) 117–134; Don Stevenson is a former managing director of Adfactory, the company that was responsible for the advertisements of SWB in the 1980s and the beginning of the 1990s (by then the brewery's name was changed into Namibia Breweries). Stevenson has also been interviewed for this book. D. Stevenson, "The Mysterious Demographics of Beer Drinking," in: G. Miescher, L. Rizzo and J. Silvester (eds.), *Posters in Action* (Basel 2009) 103.

[14] Ibid., 103.

Namibian state.[15] Furthermore, bars are places for political exchange, and it has been argued by anthropologists that through beer, Namibians can experience a liberated life in the new nation state.[16] Historically speaking, different groups in the Namibian society associated themselves with different kinds of beers. The white settlers, for example, adopted the 'South West beer' that existed in the 20th century as an icon of their settler identity.

The role of the breweries in Namibia has been neglected in the available literature, which is a missed opportunity because these companies were highly important throughout history.[17] More than 20 breweries were active in Namibia in the last 120 years and these businesses had to navigate their way through a continuously changing socio-political environment.[18] German, South African and Namibian governments all took an interest in the production and consumption of beer, and this raises a myriad of questions on how breweries and states interacted in the country's past and present. This book aims to shine a light on how the breweries of Namibia were developed over time and, consequently, how beer has changed from an icon of separated beer markets to a symbol of an independent Namibia.

---

[15] S. van Wolputte, 'Beers and Bullets, Beads and Bulls. Drink and the Making of Margins in a Small Namibian Towns', in: S. van Wolputte and M. Fumanti (eds.), *Beer in Africa: Drinking Spaces, States and Selves* (Münster 2010) 79–105.

[16] G. Dobler, 'License to Drink. Between Liberation and Inebriation in Northern Namibia', in: S. van Wolputte and M. Fumanti (eds.), *Beer in Africa: Drinking Spaces, States and Selves* (Münster 2010) 167–191.

[17] It is interesting to note that, in contrast to NBL (the dominant brewery in Namibia), the history of other major African breweries has been documented in books. NBL's main rival, SAB, is an example, see A. Mager, *Beer, Sociability and Masculinity in South Africa* (Bloomington 2010). Heineken, another major brewing concern with activities in Africa, is another example: O. van Beemen, *Heineken in Afrika* (Amsterdam 2016). Heineken is one of the largest brewing concerns active in Africa, and Van Beemen discusses its activities all over the continent, but unfortunately excludes Namibia. Heineken has a minority shareholding in Namibia Breweries, which is discussed in the third chapter of this book. For a report specifically on Heineken's presence in the Democratic Republic of Congo, see: P. Schouten., 'Brewing security? Heineken's engagement with commercial conflict-dependent actors in the Eastern DRC', *CCDA Project Report* (2013). Nigeria Breweries is featured in a special celebratory book about its own history: Y. Ogunbiyi, *Sixty years of winning with Nigeria: the history of Nigerian breweries plc 1946–2006* (Ibadan 2007).

[18] An immeasurable number of home brewers existed alongside the 'formal' commercial breweries. Most commercial breweries are discussed in this book. The best-known companies are obviously NBL and Hansa Brewery, the two largest brewing concerns. The total number of twenty breweries is reached when one takes into account the following: a number of breweries existed before the formation of NBL in 1920 and that during the apartheid era every township had a municipal beer hall and this beer was probably brewed on location. More recently, smaller companies such as Camelthorn Brewery and the Swakopmund Brewing Company emerged and SABMiller now also has a brewery located in Okahandja, Namibia.

The Research Project

This book is based on the research project "Brewing Identity: Beer and the Establishment of the Namibian Nation," conducted between 2015–2016 at the African Studies Centre Leiden (an inter-faculty institute of Leiden University) in the Netherlands.[19] Most of the information was gathered during six months of fieldwork in Namibia and South Africa. Archival research was conducted in four public archives: the National Archives and Library of Namibia, the Namibia Scientific Society, the Scientific Society Swakopmund (also known as the Sam Cohen Library), all in Namibia, and the Western Cape Archives and Records Service in Cape Town, South Africa. The data comprised colonial laws, letters, books, recipes, reports, advertisements, government policies and more. The discovery of unique files that have never been used before in academic publications greatly enriched this book.

A company archive of NBL was unfortunately not available. Employees recalled that many documents were lost during the migration of the brewery in the 1980s and there is not a current working archive.[20] A few personal archives were consulted, resulting in an interesting collection of photos, contracts and stories.[21] A lot of Namibian history can still be found in people's homes and minds. My appreciation goes to the people who were so kind to share their personal documents and stories.

The documents in the consulted archives were valuable in terms of information, but in history not everything is written down (or made available to researchers). Hence, interviews with key actors in the brewing industry proved to be indispensable. Twelve interviews were held with former and current employees from NBL, SABMiller Namibia[22], Hansa Brewery, Camelthorn Brewery and the Swakopmund Brewing Company. In addition, three interviews used were conducted by Brenda Bravenboer. It was a great opportunity to be able to make use of these interviews.

Lastly, visual material played a major role in understanding Namibia's beer history. "Visual" is meant in the broad sense of the term and this material is used to supplement

---

[19] T.A. van der Hoog, Brewing Identity: Beer and the Establishment of the Namibian Nation (unpublished MA thesis, 2016), Leiden University, Leiden.
[20] Interview Brenda Bravenboer with Ernst Ender, 22nd May 2015, and other informants during informal talks.
[21] On the difference between public and private archives in Africa: N. Mnjama, 'Using Archival Sources for Research in Africa', in: L.O. Aina, 'Introduction to Research', in: L.O. Aine (ed.), *Research in Information Sciences: An African Perspective* (Ibadan 2002) 128–129.
[22] The global brewing industry is developing in a rapid way. During my main period of fieldwork for this research project (2015–2016) I conducted interviews with employees from SABMiller Namibia. At that particular time, SABMiller was preparing a merger with Anheuser-Busch InBev. The merger was completed in late 2016 and SABMiller ceased to exist. In the book I also use the term South African Breweries (the predecessor of SABMiller) when (historically) appropriate.

the written and oral data. The most important subcategory is a collection of archival and private photos.[23] Posters similarly contain a wealth of information.[24] Beer labels indicate which brands existed in the past and which image each brand wanted to bring forth. Finally, beer bottles and mugs are carefully examined artefacts. In some cases, for example in case of the Omaruru brewery (described in Chapter One), a wooden mug is one of the rare pieces of information. The wooden mug was discovered by accident during research I undertook in Swakopmund, while drinking a beer in one of the bars in the coastal town.

The use of language is an issue that must be considered. Throughout the text, several terms of the apartheid era are used such as "Ovamboland," "kaffir beer," "natives" and "coloureds." Gregor Dobler says that "[w]hen writing about the apartheid era it is sometimes unavoidable to use terms that were important instruments of Apartheid policy." These terms describe the realities of life under a colonial government.[25] Therefore, such terms are used in the book when applicable.

---

[23] Much inspiration is taken from the work on Namibian photographs by W. Hartmann, J. Silvester and P. Hayes. The editors argue that most researchers in Africa's social history have limited interaction with photographs. In the case of Namibia, many photos of the National Archives do not even reach the "highly skilled and professional" researchers, let alone the general public. The aim of this book is to give credit to the photos acquired during the fieldwork. W. Hartmann, J. Silvester and P. Hayes (eds.), *The colonising camera: Photographs in the making of Namibian History* (Cape Town 1998).

[24] Tremendously interesting research has been done on the role of marketing in the African liquor market. See e.g.: S.J. Britten, *One nation, one beer: The mythology of the new South Africa in advertising* (unpublished PhD thesis, 2006), University of Witwatersrand, Johannesburg; D. van den Bersselaar, 'Who belongs to the 'Star people'?: negotiating beer and gin advertisements in West Africa, 1949–1975', *The Journal of African History* Vol. 52 No. 3 (2011) 385–408; A. Mager, *Beer, Sociability and Masculinity in South Africa* (Bloomington 2010).

[25] G. Dobler, *Traders and Trade in Colonial Ovamboland: Elite Formation and the Politics of Consumption under Indirect Rule and Apartheid, 1925–1990* (Basel 2014) XXII–XXIII.

Prelude: A Centuries-long Tradition of Home Brewing

Namibia has a centuries-long tradition of home brewing, in which beer is a key drink. The idea that the history of beer brewing in Namibia only commenced with the arrival of European settlers is historically incorrect. Long before the establishment of formal brewing companies, the peoples who lived in the area that is now Namibia were involved in the brewing of beer.[26] More often than not these brews are described today as "traditional," to distinguish them from bottled European-style beers. Other forms of alcohol were also produced, such as wine- and brandy-like beverages. In order to counterbalance a narrow view on the commercial beer market that emerged in the 20th century, this Prelude elaborates on the various cultures of home brewing in Namibia.

Virtually all ethnic groups in Namibia have rich drinking cultures. An important source of information on these phenomena are reports of foreign travellers and missionaries, who visited the south-western part of Africa prior to the establishment of the German Protectorate in 1884.[27] In search of adventure, religion or fortune, they stumbled upon ethnic groups and their beer making rituals. The historian Jeremy Silvester noted that already in 1779, the European explorer Hendrik Wikar, who was employed by the Dutch East India Company for a few years, encountered a San family who had gathered around a pot of beer. This is perhaps the earliest written notion of the existence of beer in Namibia. However, beer was certainly brewed in the region even before this encounter. Other European accounts followed and often gave vivid descriptions of the drinking cultures that existed.[28]

An exceptionally detailed, although short, description of the Herero and Nama drinking culture was written by Heinrich Vedder, a well-known missionary and ethnographer.[29] Historians need to treat his work with care, as is the case with all historical sources:

---

[26] For more information on pre-colonial Namibia, see M. Wallace, *A History of Namibia: From the Beginning to 1990* (Cape Town 2011) 1–131.

[27] Among them are T. Baines, *Explorations in South West Africa* (London 1864); V. Forbes, *Anders Sparrman Travels in the Cape 1772–76* (Cape Town 1975); V. Forbes, *Travels and Adventures in Southern Africa by George Thompson* (Cape Town 1968); H. Waterhouse, *Simon van der Stel's Journal of his Expedition to Namaqualand, 1685–6* (London 1932); I. Rudner and J. Rudner, *Axel Wilhelm Eriksson of Hereroland (1846–1901): His Life and Letters* (Windhoek 2006).

[28] NAN, F002-NAMZ 0559, J. Silvester, A trail of broken beer bottles, the Namibian Weekender, 10/09/99.

[29] NSS, H. Vedder, 'Notes on the Brewing of Kaffir Beer in S.W.A.: A History of Beer', Journal of the South West Africa Scientific Society, Vol. 3 (1951) 41–43. Vedder's most important work is H. Vedder, *Das alte Südwestafrika: Die Geschichte Südwestafrikas bis zum Tode Maharero 1890* (Berlin reprint 1985). Originally published in 1934.

Jan-Bart Gewald, Brigitte Lau and Jill Kinahan have argued convincingly that Vedder's work is loaded with colonial prejudice.[30] An example of this prejudice is his claim that the Herero Revolt was partially caused by "the fact that the paramount chief of the Herero was a drunkard" — academic studies have proven that the revolt was started for distinct other reasons.[31] That does not mean that all of Vedder's ethnographic observations are immediately useless: his writings contain rare and valuable pieces of information on a time period that is not well covered in written documents.

Interesting is that according to Vedder, the Herero supposedly did not a have a drinking culture: the Nama introduced the intoxicating honey-beer to the Herero when an alliance was formed by the Nama chief Jonker Afrikaner and the Herero chief Kahitjene. Before this, the Nama tried to secure their secret by guarding stocks of wild honey. The increasing demand caused a shortage of this valuable ingredient and sugar was used as a substitute. Sugar is now called *danib*, which means honey. Traders from Cape Town brought sugar to Jonker Afrikaner, who received the precious commodity in return for cattle. A long-distance trade with alcohol as a key factor was the result.[32]

Beer played a central part in the "culture and diet" of the Oshivambo-speaking group, according to botanist Robert Rodin.[33] Anthropologist Hermann Tönjes, who spent nine years among the Ovambo at the start of the 20th century, describes beer (*omalodu*) as the "most important beverage" of the ethnic groups that comprised the Oshivambo.[34] Ovamboland became the colonial name of an administrative area in the northern part of South West Africa. The territory describes several polities whose inhabitants spoke closely related languages, collectively called the Oshivambo or Oshiwambo.[35] These inhabitants

---

[30] See the work of Jan-Bart Gewald, Brigitte Lau and Jill Kinahan in J.B. Gewald, *Herero Heroes: A Socio-Political History of the Herero of Namibia 1890–1923* (Oxford 1999) 5–6. Grotpeter provides a short background of Vedder and pointed out his "pro-German missionary prejudice." J.J. Grotpeter, *Historical Dictionary of Namibia* (Metuchen 1994) 552–553.

[31] The quote comes from: NSS, H. Vedder, 'Notes on the Brewing of Kaffir Beer in S.W.A.: A History of Beer', Journal of the South West Africa Scientific Society, Vol. 3 (1951) 41–43. For an academic explanation of the Herero Revolt see J.B. Gewald, *Herero Heroes: A Socio-Political History of the Herero of Namibia 1890–1923* (Oxford 1999).

[32] NSS, H. Vedder, 'Notes on the Brewing of Kaffir Beer in S.W.A.: A History of Beer', Journal of the South West Africa Scientific Society, Vol. 3 (1951) 41–43.

[33] Rodin provides an extensive overview of the plants that are used by the Ovambo, and made an interesting comment by writing that the complex malting process is "one of the evidences that a so-called primitive people are really not so." R.J. Rodin, *The Ethnobotany of the Kwanyama Ovambos* (Lawrence 1985).

[34] Tönjes gives detailed descriptions of how the beers are made and concludes that the brews "will please a European's palate." H. Tönjes, *Ovamboland* (Windhoek 1996) 74–76. The first edition was published in German in 1911.

[35] G. Dobler, *Traders and Trade in Colonial Ovamboland: Elite Formation and the Politics of Consumption under Indirect Rule and Apartheid, 1925–1990* (Basel 2014) XIX. Dobler provides a comprehensive historical overview of Ovamboland. Half of the population of Namibia lives in Ovamboland and this

Fig. 2: Two young women holding beer pots on their heads in Ovamboland, 1930.

made various kinds of beers, such as *omalodu* (also called "kaffir beer" by the colonial authorities[36]), *oshikundu*[37] ("rough beer") and *omanyeu* ("lighter beer"). Rodin describes how the "rather complicated malting process" was in use for hundreds of years before Europeans entered the area and that many households brewed beer daily.[38]

A few recipes have survived the test of time and show the ingenuity of those brewers under rough circumstances. The term "beer" is herein used as a wide category of beer-like, low alcoholic substances. All sorts of ingredients with the ability to ferment were used: honey, sugar, fruit, mealie-meal, Boer-meal, corn and beans are examples.[39] Honey

---

region played therefore a crucial role in the development of the commercial beer market. The third chapter deals with this topic. For a history on the Ovambo kingdoms see F. N. Williams, *Precolonial Communities of Southwestern Africa: A History of Owambo Kingdoms 1600–1920* (Windhoek 1991).

[36] "Kaffir" is a derogatory term used to describe the local population. The term "kaffir beer" was widely used by the South African administration. In this case, the description comes from Rodin.

[37] For a contemporary study on *oshikundu*, see W. Embashu et al., 'Processing methods of Oshikundu, a traditional beverage from sub-tribes within Aawambo culture in the Northern Namibia', *Journal for Studies in Humanities and Social Sciences* Vol. 2 No. 1 (2013) 117–127.

[38] R.J. Rodin, *The Ethnobotany of the Kwanyama Ovambos* (Lawrence 1985).

[39] NSS, H. Vedder, 'Notes on the Brewing of Kaffir Beer in S.W.A.: A History of Beer', *Journal of the South West Africa Scientific Society*, Vol. 3 (1951) 41–43.; NAN, F002-NAMZ 0559, J. Silvester, A trail of broken beer bottles, the Namibian Weekender, 10/09/99, NAN, F002-RARA/062, Native beverages 1931.

beer was widespread in southern and central Namibia, but other forms also existed, such as sugar beer.[40] Contrary to the practice of modern day breweries, the brewers in the aforementioned communities were and still are predominantly female.[41] Beer is a highly gendered drink.[42] It was very important that every household had a sufficient quantity of beer available. Beer was probably the most prevalent, but certainly not the only alcoholic beverage to be found in the region. Other drinks include wine made of various fruits (*omavinju*), brandy (*olambika*), mead (*lafaula*) and palm wine (according to ethnobotanist Rodin palm wine was also called *omavinju*). While the majority of the available source material deals with the Ovambo, other groups also made several forms of liquor. The Oorlam community for instance, made brandy.[43]

A recipe for sugar beer, written down by the German missionary Vedder, gives an idea of the creativity that was involved in brewing. According to Vedder, this beer was brewed by several groups, including the Herero and Nama. The recipes highlights ingredients such as peas and potatoes, and brewing equipment such as animal skins and the earth:

> In a suitable receptacle (barrel, paraffin tin, etc.) 4–10 lbs. of sugar are mixed with a few pounds of peas and about ten potatoes cut into small bits in hot water. Cold water is then added until the receptacle is filled with lukewarm water. This mixture is made to ferment

---

[40] NAN, F002-NAMZ 0559, J. Silvester, A trail of broken beer bottles, the Namibian Weekender, 10/09/99.

[41] NSS, H. Vedder, 'Notes on the Brewing of Kaffir Beer in S.W.A.: A History of Beer', *Journal of the South West Africa Scientific Society*, Vol. 3 (1951) 41–43.; NAN, F002-NAMZ 0559, J. Silvester, A trail of broken beer bottles, the Namibian Weekender, 10/09/99; NAN, F002-RARA/062, Native beverages 1931.

[42] Tönjes writes for example that all brewers in Ovamboland were women, based on anthropological studies around 1900. H. Tönjes, *Ovamboland* (Windhoek 1996) 74–76. Several contemporary scholars dealt with the idea that beer can make a nation gendered. Van Beek argues for instance that among the Kapsiki, beer constitutes a male-dominated discourse, but that local beer is often brewed by women. W. van Beek, 'Kapsiki beer dynamics', in: C. Raimond, E. Garine and O. Langlois (eds.), *Ressouces vivriéres et choix alimentaires dans le basin du Tchad* (Paris 2005) 477–499. Mager focuses the connection between beer and masculinity in South Africa. A. Mager, *Beer, Sociability and Masculinity in South Africa* (Bloomington 2010). Similarly, Fumanti argues that beer is a way for Namibian males to show their masculinity. M. Fumanti, '"I Like My Windhoek Lager": Beer Consumption and the Making of Men in Namibia', in: S. van Wolputte and M. Fumanti (eds.), *Beer in Africa: Drinking Spaces, States and Selves* (Münster 2010) 257–274. Stevenson recognises that in the advertisement of SWB/NBL the beer drinkers were mainly male and depicted in different social spaces. The marketing showed a hunter drinking a seasonal dark beer, African men plying football, and — for a change — a man embraced by two attractive women. In the words of Stevenson, "[t]he posters […] draw on male fantasies and connect them to specific brands." D. Stevenson,"The Mysterious Demographics of Beer Drinking," in: G. Miescher, L. Rizzo and J. Silvester (eds.), *Posters in Action* (Basel 2009) 106–107.

[43] R.J. Rodin, *The Ethnobotany of the Kwanyama Ovambos* (Lawrence 1985); NAN, F002-NAMZ 0559, J. Silvester, A trail of broken beer bottles, the Namibian Weekender, 10/09/99; NAN, F002-RARA/062, Native beverages 1931.

by keeping the receptacle warm with skins and blankets or by burying it in the earth to escape detection, until it has lost its taste of sugar.[44]

There were multiple reasons for drinking beer. Importantly, home brewed beer was a relatively healthy drink. Rodin describes the beer of the Ovambo as "very nutritious and an important dietary component."[45] Furthermore, it was used as a way of dealing with a poor quality of water[46], similar to the practices in medieval Europe, where parts of the population drank low-alcoholic beer on a daily basis. But the production and consumption of beer also had an important ritualistic function, something which is also recognised in societies in other parts of the African continent.[47]

It is important to note that these traditions are still being carried on today. The advent of modern breweries with mass-scale production in the 20th century did not erase the existence of homemade beer, although the methods and ingredients used may have changed over time. It is estimated that the local brewing of beer still forms a major part of the contemporary Namibian liquor market, although it is difficult to measure this. Especially the country's rural areas probably have a lively home brewing culture, but even in Katatura, the township of Windhoek where an estimated 60% of the city's population live, drinks like *tombo* are available.[48] Namibian home brewing would be a perfect topic for future research.

The reason this Prelude was added is to clarify that home brewing is a crucial part of the Namibian beer market. It is correct to say that NBL dominates the Namibian beer market today, insofar one speaks about the commercial (formal) beer market. Namibians have been home brewing beer for centuries and are still doing so. A substantial part of the actual beer market consists of these homebrews and forms a vital part of Namibian societies. Home brewing will be mentioned again in this book because of the importance of this phenomenon.

---

[44] NSS, H. Vedder, 'Notes on the Brewing of Kaffir Beer in S.W.A.: A History of Beer', *Journal of the South West Africa Scientific Society*, Vol. 3 (1951) 41-43. More recipes can be found in the second appendix of this book.
[45] R.J. Rodin, *The Ethnobotany of the Kwanyama Ovambos* (Lawrence 1985).
[46] NAN, F002-NAMZ 0559, J. Silvester, A trail of broken beer bottles, the Namibian Weekender, 10/09/99.
[47] I. de Garine and V. de Garine (eds.), *Drinking: Anthropological Approaches* (New York 2001); M. Douglas (ed.), *Constructive Drinking: Perspectives on Drink from Anthropology* (Cambridge 1987); H. Hahn, 'Consumption, Identities and Agency in Africa: Introduction', in: Hahn, H. (ed.), *Consumption in Africa: Anthropological Approaches* (Berlin 2008) 9–42.
[48] *Tombo* is a very strong home brewed drink. *Oshikundu* and other brews are also easily accessible.

1 The Advent of Formal Breweries, 1900–1920

For the past hundred years, the Namibian beer market has for a large part been influenced by the existence of NBL, the famous brewing company that produces classic brews such as Windhoek Lager and Tafel Lager. Lesser known is the elaborate brewing history that existed before the formation of NBL and involved the founding of the very first brewing companies in the country. This chapter demonstrates how the commercial beer market emerged at the beginning of the 20th century, zooming in on some of the earliest companies and pioneering settlers that were able to brew beer and sell it to their fellow settlers. Some of these stories have been 'lost' in the archives for decades but are now finally brought to light again. They are hereby combined into the first attempt to provide a general narrative of how the beer industry developed over time in Namibia.

The Arrival of European Settlers

The area that is modern Namibia saw a vast influx of European settlers after the establishment of the German Protectorate in 1884. During the Berlin Conference of 1884–1885 the colonisation of Africa was regulated by the European superpowers. This so-called "Scramble for Africa" resulted in the division of the African continent between a few major countries. Germany also felt the desire to become an imperial power and hence claimed "German South West Africa" (GSWA) for itself. Already long before this conference, European traders and explorers had set foot on the coast of the south-western part of Africa. The claims of the German government were however finalised with the outcome of the Berlin Conference, making the area an official Protectorate. This conference is the reason why the eastern border of Namibia is an almost perfect straight line – according to some accounts, the European diplomats used a ruler to draw straight lines on the continental map of Africa.[1] The borders of GSWA are almost the same as contemporary Namibia, with an important exception of the port Walvis Bay, which was British territory at that time.[2]

---

[1] All standard works on African history deal with the "Scramble for Africa." A starting point is J.D. Fage, *A History of Africa* (London 1988).

[2] M. Wallace, *A History of Namibia: From the Beginning to 1990* (Cape Town 2011) 9; P. Hayes et al., *Namibia under South African Rule: Mobility and Containment 1915–46* (Oxford 1988) 3; for a specific work on another highly contested area see B. Kangumu, *Contesting Caprivi: A History of Colonial Isolation and Regional Nationalism in Namibia* (Basel 2011).

Fig. 3: Imported beer bottles from Germany, currently displayed in the Swakopmund Museum.

German and other European settlers quickly began setting up an administration in the stretch of land that was still largely unknown to them. A colonial bureaucracy, the *Schutztruppe* (military forces), and pioneering families came to the colony to start a new life. All sorts of goods were imported from overseas to help build houses, railways, water works, and more. The steamers from the Woermann Line transported a wide variety of goods to the shores of GSWA: building materials, horses, rifles, and also beer.

Nowadays, one can regularly find those old, imported beer bottles during construction work on buildings. Some climates of Namibia preserved the bottles quite well and now they have become valuable items for collectors. In a few cases the labels remained intact and reveal interesting insights into the long-distance trade from more than a century ago. The beers were produced in German cities such as Hamburg and Munich and were imported to specific places like Swakopmund and Windhoek.[3] The bottles were made of

---

[3] I would like to thank the Swakopmund Museum in Swakopmund for the opportunity to take a closer look at their bottles and to take photos. An address book from 1908 reveals that beer could be imported via various companies in Hamburg. NSS, Fitzner, R., Adressbuch für Deutsch-Südwestafrika 1908 (Ber-

thick glass to withstand the fermentation process during the lengthy sea trip while the glass was darkly coloured (black, brown or green) to block out the light, as this could disturb the maturing process of the beer.[4]

In those days, and we are talking about the end of the 19th century and the beginning of the 20th century, drinking was the main leisure activity for settler communities. Male settlers outnumbered females by two to one, and drinking beer was an important recreational activity for this group. Statistics from 1903 illustrate the heavy beer consumption. From the 167 firm licences in GSWA, 53 were concerned with alcohol — that means that one third of all business involved liquor. In Windhoek alone there was one bar for every 41 settlers, showing the overwhelming importance of such drinking places.[5]

In this respect, a complaint that was discussed in newspapers (although a bit later in time) is exemplary. Attention was given to a phenomenon that was aptly called "Windhoekeritis"; meaning the habits of drinking, gambling and prostitution, which apparently spread like a disease all over the country.[6] Such words should be taken with a grain of salt, but it shows that drinking formed a major part of daily life. Another example can be found at the coast. After diamonds were discovered in Lüderitzbucht, prospector Fred Cornell visited the area. He wrote his impressions down in the following way: "The first thing that struck me was the enormous number of empty bottles that lay piled and scattered about in all directions."[7]

After the occupation of GSWA by South African forces in 1915, the indulgence of the settlers was widely deployed in an anti-German (media) campaign. It is striking that beer (and drinking in general) became one of the vocal points of complaints against the German-speaking population. Another quote shines light on these endeavours. It should again be taken with a healthy grain of salt, but does says something about the position beer had in the early days of the Protectorate. Dr. H. F. B. Walker wrote in a newspaper:

> I believe the Germans here are heavy drinkers [...] A small place like Swakopmund had over thirty hotels and beershops. Breweries and distilleries abound [....] it would not be safe to walk anywhere in the country with bare feet, because you would cut yourself with broken glass. On the mountain-tops, in the desert or bush, you will find bottles; you see buildings and walls made of bottles and mud, garden paths and beds are ornamented with them.[8]

---

    lin 1908) XXXV.
[4] E. Lastovia and A. Lastovia, *Bottles & Bygones* (Cape Town 1982).
[5] R. Gordon, 'Inside the Windhoek Lager: Liquor and Lust in Namibia', in: W. Jankowiak and D. Bradburd (eds.) *Drugs, labor, and colonial expansion* (Tucson 2003) 124.
[6] R. Gordon, 'Inside the Windhoek Lager: Liquor and Lust in Namibia' 126.
[7] Ibid., 123.
[8] Ibid., 124.

Fig. 4: Schutztruppe soldiers in Windhoek are drinking beer.

Apparently, beer and its remnants were everywhere. The import of beer from another part of the world was however not a long-term solution to provide for the thirst of the new inhabitants of GSWA. The beer was strong and dark, as it had to withstand a long sea journey. The hot and arid climate of the colony was, to be fair, quite unsuitable for such heavy drinks.[9] Furthermore, importing goods from far away was expensive and it was difficult to predict the demand, while the delivery took a long time.[10] Soon it became clear that this situation was not sustainable, especially with a growing population. Another solution was necessary and thus the settlers were on the eve of starting their own breweries in the territory.

Any industry could however only emerge and sustain itself after towns were founded, transport roads and water works were developed and settler communities were growing. Although the German Protectorate was declared in 1884, the German rule was only firm-

---

[9] Mentioned in various NBL sources, such as NLN, 96/0511 B, Namibia Breweries Limited, 1920–1995.
[10] E. Rosenthal, *Tankards & Tradition* (Cape Town 1961) 157.

ly consolidated a mere twenty years later, after the war that occurred between 1904–1908, where German troops massacred an estimated 80% of the Herero and 60% of the Nama population.[11] It was the first genocide of the 20th century and led to the instalment of concentration camps.[12] The historian Marion Wallace convincingly argues that this genocide is of "great historical significance" for Namibia and its powerful repercussions can still be felt today.[13] Once the colonial structures were consolidated in the early 20th century, all sorts of industries were able to develop, including the beer industry.

How to Establish a Brewery

Already in 1897, a civil engineer by the name of Rehbock writes in a report on water irrigation that "the establishment of a brewery in the Protectorate is only a matter of time."[14] Rehbock was certainly right, because only a few years later several breweries sprung up all over the country. Beer consumption rose sharply following the growth of the European population, for instance through an expansion of German troops and the discovery of diamonds near Lüderitz.[15]

The exact location for these companies can be explained by an analysis of three key factors that are necessary to brew successfully. The first factor is the presence of people: a business cannot be sustained without having enough consumers in the nearby surroundings. The second factor is the availability of water as it is of extreme importance for brewing beer. Both the quantity and quality of water are also vital. The third factor is means of transport: the ability to move brewing equipment, ingredients and products around the country is crucial. An analysis of the presence of people, water and transport opportunities in those days provides a context to the story that is laid out in the remainder of this book. The geographical features of the land, especially water, influenced the presence of people, communication and thus historical events.

In this book, a distinction is made between two kinds of breweries. The first kind are informal breweries, meaning home brewers. Informal breweries provide beer for a family or a small community. The second are formal breweries, meaning registered companies that produce manufactured beers for a commercial market. The next part will focus solely on formal breweries.

---

[11] For a detailed overview, see J.B. Gewald, *Herero Heroes: A Socio-Political History of the Herero of Namibia 1890–1923* (Oxford 1999).
[12] C.W. Erichsen, *"The angel of death has descended violently among them." Concentration camps and prisoners-of-war in Namibia, 1904–08* (Leiden 2005).
[13] M. Wallace, *A History of Namibia: From the Beginning to 1990* (Cape Town 2011) 155.
[14] E. Rosenthal, *Tankards & Tradition* (Cape Town 1961) 157.
[15] Ibid., 157–158.

Consumers

GSWA had a small population that was scattered across an enormous stretch of land. Similar to other parts of Africa, the colonisation of Namibia was a slow and uneven process.[16] The judicial claims of Germany on the south-western part of Africa, formulated during the "Scramble for Africa," did not immediately match the on-site presence by settlers. Instead, the settler population grew unevenly after the Protectorate was declared. Patricia Hayes et al. argue that "Namibia is striking for the unevenness in the timing and spread of new capitalist and colonial relations." When South Africa took over the German administration, the colonial state was still "ill-informed and weak." In a period of thirty years, the "state had consolidated itself to a considerable degree."[17] The first full scale census of the South African administration dates back to 1920 and gives a comprehensive overview of the population.[18] Population statistics from before this date are however rare and difficult to obtain.[19]

We do have a few documents that give an impression of the size of the settler communities in the early days of GSWA. An example is an overview of the district of Otjimbingwe from 1896, roughly a decade after the establishment of the German colony and a few years before the first breweries were founded. 339 white settlers lived in this district that contained some of the most important towns of GSWA, including Swakopmund, Omaruru and Otjimbingwe.[20] While this picture does not account for the subsequent population growth and is therefore not representative of the white population between 1900–1920, it underlines the claim that the territory had a small and scattered white population. This is due to two other factors that are described below: the low availability of water and the sheer size of the country.

Water

Access to water is fundamental for survival and in the history of Namibia, human movement and settlement has always been strained due to the limited availability of water.[21]

---

[16] T.B. Hansen, and F. Stepputat, 'Sovereignty Revisited', *Annual Review of Anthropology* Vol. 35 (2006) 296; P. Hayes et al., *Namibia under South African Rule: Mobility and Containment 1915–46* (Oxford 1988) 4.

[17] Ibid.

[18] NSS, Territory of South-West Africa, Report on the Census of the European Population, taken on the 3rd May, 1921; NSS, Territory of South West Africa, Report on the Census of the European Population, taken on the 4th May, 1926.

[19] More research is necessary to provide a clear picture. A starting point could be the address books in the collection of the Namibia Scientific Society (from 1908 to the 1930s), which contain bits of information on the population.

[20] NSS, A. Bourquin, *Omaruru: Die Geschichte einer Stadt* (unpublished, 1969) 54.

[21] P. Heyns et al., *Namibia's Water* 50; G. Christelis, and Wilhelm Struckmeier (eds.), *Groundwater in Namibia, an explanation to the Hydrogeological Map* (Windhoek 2001) 11; 23–24; 43; 46; 57; 157.

Fig. 5: A group of influential settlers sitting outside a house and drinking beer, seated: Duft and Von Lindequist, standing left to right: Nitzsche, Von Goldammer, Gustav Voigts, Wecke, Paul Richter, Wasmannsdorf, Gutsche, Richard Voigts. The photo was taken in 1898.

In pre-colonial times, people relied on surface- and rainwater, springs, wells and cisterns. In the 19th century, permanent settlements emerged, places that have now grown into modern towns. All of these places were close to rain- and groundwater supplies.[22] The first dams were built by missionaries, the very first was probably erected in the 1850s.[23] One of the key tasks of the German colonial administration was subsequently to harness and develop the water supplies.[24] The influx of settlers resulted in the expropriation of land from African owners and the emergence of towns.

An infrastructure was necessary to support colonial trade and administration, but the existing water supply was by far not sustainable when the settler economy emerged.[25] Dams were constructed, aquifers tapped, and with the introduction of drilled boreholes in the

---

[22] B. Lau and C. Sterk, *Namibian Water Resources and their Management: A Preliminary History*, ARCHEIA No. 15 (Windhoek 1990) 4.
[23] Ibid., 26.
[24] P. Heyns et al., *Namibia's Water, A Decision Makers' Guide* (Windhoek 1998) 159.
[25] B. Lau and C. Sterk, *Namibian Water Resources and their Management: A Preliminary History*, ARCHEIA No. 15 (Windhoek 1990) 5.

late 1800s and early 1900s, deep groundwater could be extracted.[26] Before 1906, the borehole drilling happened on an ad hoc basis. This changed in 1906, when the drilling activities were centralised by the government.[27] The water that was supplied by boreholes remained the major water source in the German era.[28] Plans were made to build dams, as dams were the key factor in the German water management policy.[29] The efforts of the colonial government made sense, as Namibia is the driest country south of the Sahara. Hence, water drastically impacts where and how people live.[30]

Transport
Because of the sheer size of the country, mobility was always a central theme throughout Namibia's history. Namibia is the world's thirty-fourth largest country but has, due to the harsh climatological conditions, a limited number of inhabitants. Even today Namibia is, after Mongolia, the least densely populated country in the world.[31] More than a hundred years ago, during the German era, the population was even smaller. The settlers entered an enormous stretch of land with a great variety of geographical features, including the oldest desert in the world, high mountains, wide stretches of savanna and a delta in the north. Settlers often travelled by ox wagons or horses, using bad and dusty roads. The army even had a department with camel riders, while indigenous young men working for the postal service transported the mail by foot, crossing large distances. Eventually, the train (and later, the car) was introduced to the territory, making it much easier to transport goods and people.[32]

As soon as the European settlers settled down, towns emerged and trade developed, a whole range of breweries popped up seemingly out of nowhere. The archival research of this book project shows that all over the country breweries were built. Beer was not limited to well-known places such as Windhoek. Presumably, not all companies were properly recorded in the archives, which means that it is likely that even more breweries saw the light of day than we are currently aware of. An interesting aspect of the emerging brewing culture was the existence of small-scale "Weissbier" brewers, who supposedly

---

[26] P. Heyns et al., *Namibia's Water, A Decision Makers' Guide* (Windhoek 1998) 159.
[27] B. Lau and C. Sterk, *Namibian Water Resources and their Management: A Preliminary History*, ARCHEIA No. 15 (Windhoek 1990) 63.
[28] Ibid., 6.
[29] Ibid., 26.
[30] P. Heyns et al., *Namibia's Water, A Decision Makers' Guide* (Windhoek 1998) 45; G. Christelis, and Wilhelm Struckmeier (eds.), *Groundwater in Namibia, an explanation to the Hydrogeological Map* (Windhoek 2001) 6.
[31] World Population Review 2019, www.worldpopulationreview.com/countries/namibia-population (accessed on the 17th April 2019).
[32] U. Jäschke and B. Bravenboer (eds.), *History of the Namibian road sector* (Windhoek 2011).

were active in almost every town of GSWA. However, written sources on this topic are rare and therefore this work does not deal with them.

In this book, the so-called "beer triangle" is essential, with its three major brewing towns: Swakopmund, Windhoek and Omaruru. The following paragraph describes these brewing towns in more detail. Besides the companies that were founded in the triangle, a whole range of other breweries were established in GSWA during the first decades of the 20th century. In the northern part of the territory, breweries existed in Otavi[33] and Grootfontein[34]. In the central part of the territory, Karibib[35], Okahandja[36] and Rehoboth[37] each had a brewery. In the southern part of the territory, Lüderitz[38] and Keetmanshoop[39] established themselves as brewing towns, and as Chapters Two and Three will show, new breweries emerged in time.

The Beer Triangle

In the early 1900s, three places in GSWA developed into influential brewing towns: Swakopmund, Omaruru and Windhoek. The three towns are all part of the Central Na-

---

[33] A brewery existed in Otavi in 1906, although its name is unknown. According to Freyer, a man named Karl Knatz was the owner of a hotel and a brewery in town. See E.P.W. Freyer, *Chronik von Otavi und Umgebung 1906–1966* (Windhoek 1966) 35.

[34] Based on a photo we can tell that the brewery was located in or near Grootfontein. NSS, Brauerei — Blick über den Staudamm der Farm Gemsbocklaagte auf einen Schweinekoben (links) und eine Brauerei (rechts) 1448/11/J11.

[35] In Karibib, a town on the Kahn River between Swakopmund and Windhoek, an address book mentions a Bierbrauerei and Selterwasserfabrik belonging to H. Kahl in 1908. Furthermore, the Karibiber Brauerei und Mineralwasserfabrik existed in 1912. The director was Carl Hanke. NSS, Fitzner, R., Adressbuch für Deutsch-Südwestafrika 1908 (Berlin 1908) 51; SSS, 2004.115.2, Rechnung der Brauerei Hanke in Karibib and Herr Hier.

[36] In Okahandja, a brewery was owned by C. Bauer. It is uncertain whether this is the same Mr. Bauer who started one of the largest breweries in Windhoek. NSS, Fitzner, R., Adressbuch für Deutsch-Südwestafrika 1908 (Berlin 1908) 64.

[37] In Rehoboth a brewery owned by Breckwoldt & Müller existed. NSS, Fitzner, R., Adressbuch für Deutsch-Südwestafrika 1908 (Berlin 1908) 78.

[38] The coastal town Lüderitzbucht also had a brewery, owned by Johannes Osbahr. He also owned the brewery in Keetmanshoop. NSS, Fitzner, R., Adressbuch für Deutsch-Südwestafrika 1908 (Berlin 1908) 59.

[39] In 1908, Osbahr is mentioned as the owner of the brewery in Keetmanshoop. Karl Fischer established a brewery in the same town in 1911: the Bürgerliches Brauhaus G.m.b.H., also known as the Keetmanshooper Brauerei und Mineralwasser Fabrik Karl Fischer & Co. It is unclear if the two companies were the same or in fact two separate ones. In the previous year, an ice-making factory opened its doors, which was part of the brewery. Mr. Fischer brewed Weissbier which apparently was a success: according to the source material, a part of the Brauhaus was turned into a beer garden, called The Garden Café. NSS, Fitzner, R., Adressbuch für Deutsch-Südwestafrika 1908 (Berlin 1908) 53; SSS, 2004.115.26, Brewery Historical Information – How it was established in Keetmanshoop. A brewery in Keetmanshoop is also mentioned in the report of the Chamber of Commerce: NSS, Jahresbericht der Windhuker Handelskammer 1913.

mib-Windhoek area and share an interwoven history.[40] The largest brewing companies of the beer triangle merged in 1920 into South West Breweries (SWB), the predecessor of NBL.[41] In this way their legacy is still tangible today, as they are united in the single company that dominated the national brewing market during the last century. The surprising stories of these pioneering brewers have long remained hidden because they were never written down. For the sake of history, this book highlights the distinct stories of these brewing towns until 1920, the year of the merger.

Swakopmund: The Beginning
Swakopmund, the picturesque costal town, formed the beginning of the commercial brewing industry in Namibia. Nowadays, it is mostly a quiet place where visitors can enjoy German architecture and sea food, but back then, Swakopmund had the hustle and bustle of an important harbour that formed the starting point of many colonial endeavours. The coastal town was founded in 1892 as the harbour for GSWA.[42] The already existing harbour in Walvis Bay was British territory and therefore the German colonial administration was not able to use it. Through Swakopmund, the building materials for houses and roads, many necessities for daily life and the settlers themselves entered the territory for the first time. The name of Swakopmund is a combination of the bastardised Nama name *Tsoachaub* [the original name for this place] and the German word *Mund* [mouth].[43]

The very first formal brewery of Namibia established by settlers was most probably Rudolph Jauch's Swakopmunder Brauerei.[44] The company opened its doors in early 1900 and sold the beer "Bavaria-Bräu." One source mentions the 1st February as the starting date[45], while another source mentions the 25th February.[46] While the exact date remains uncertain, we can safely assume that the brewery started its operations in the beginning of 1900 because Luitpold, Prince Regent of Bavaria sent a congratulatory telegram for the opening.[47]

---

[40] The term "beer triangle" is coined because of their triangular connection on the map and the joint role they play in the history of GSWA. Identifying triangles is not uncommon: Grootfontein, Otavi and Tsumeb form for example the so-called "maize triangle." P. Heyns et al., *Namibia's Water, A Decision Makers' Guide* (Windhoek 1998) 77.
[41] Ibid., 28.
[42] For more on Swakopmund, see: H. Rautenberg, *Das alte Swakopmund: 1892–1919* (Swakopmund 1967); Scientific Society Swakopmund, *Swakopmund: Eine kleine Chronik* (Swakopmund 2006); C. von Dewitz, *Swakopmund: Der kleine Stadtführer* (Windhoek 2009).
[43] A.P.J. Albertyn, *Die Ensiklopedie Van Name In Suidwes-Afrika* (Pretoria 1984) 95.
[44] SSS, 2004.19.59, Anzeigen: Ein guter Spiegel der damaligen Wirtschaftslage.
[45] H. Rautenberg, *Das alte Swakopmund: 1892–1919* (Swakopmund 1967) 152.
[46] SSS, 2000.1.702, Hundert Jahre Südwestafrika.
[47] Ibid.

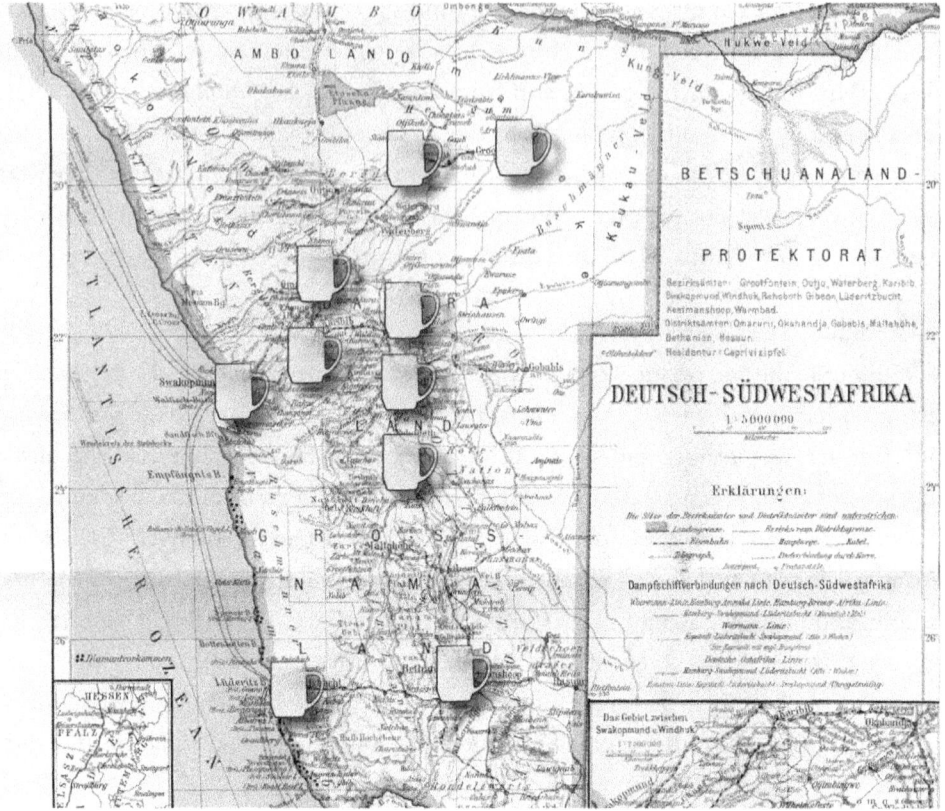

Fig. 6: A map with all known brewing towns prior to 1920. Some towns had more than one brewery.

Newspaper advertisements of 1901 promoted their Berliner-style Weissbier and dunkles Bier (dark beer), products that are suitable for transport from Swakopmund into the interior of the country.[48] In 1902, Hermann Dietz announced to all the "Inhabitants of Swakopmund and travellers passing through" that he had started serving beer from the "Weissbier-Brauerei" in the Hotel Germania. The hotel was situated next to the brewery.[49] An overview of companies in Swakopmund from 1902 shows that the company was listed as a beer brewery and employed two white and seven coloured people.[50] What eventually happened with the Swakopmunder Brauerei is uncertain, as the available records do not include any further information.[51]

---

[48] SSS, 2004.19.59, Anzeigen: Ein guter Spiegel der damaligen Wirtschaftslage.
[49] SSS, 2000.1.860, Geschäfts-Eröffnung; H. Rautenberg, *Das alte Swakopmund: 1892–1919* (Swakopmund 1967) 152.
[50] Ibid., 155.
[51] A directory from 1908 mentions the founding of a brewery in 1905 ("Brauereigesellschaft Swakopmund, G.m.b.H"), and the existence of two breweries in 1908: "Bierbrauereien: Brauereigesellschaft Swakopmund, G.m.b.H. (Heinrich Eggert, Geschäftsführer; Engelbert de Fries, Stellvertreter); Fischer

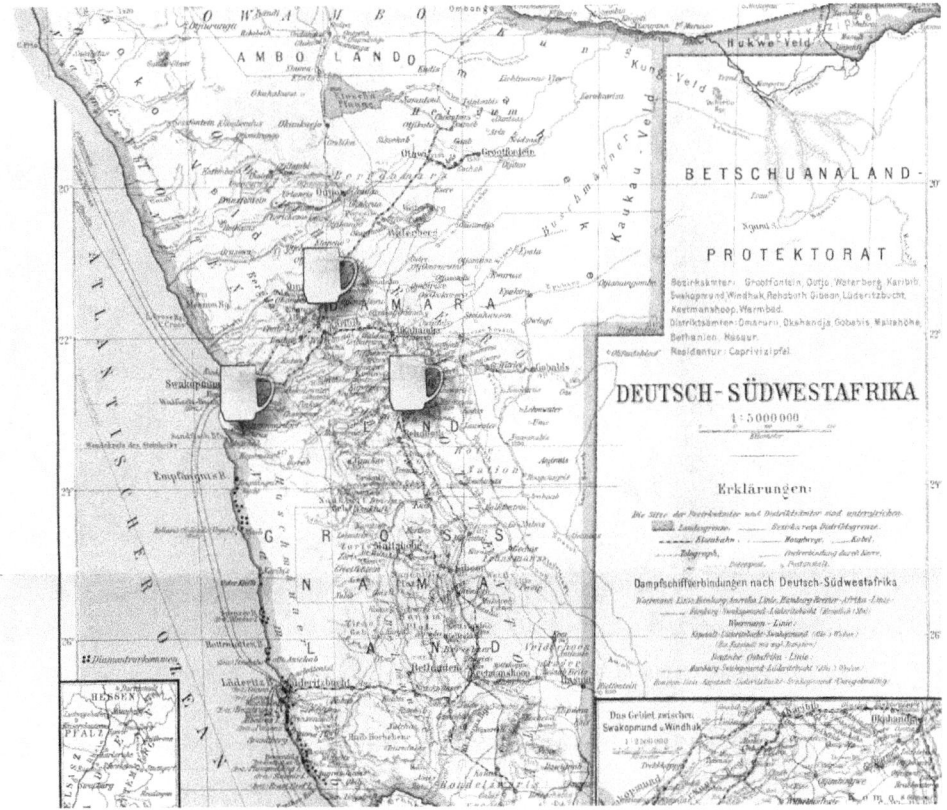

Fig. 7: The beer triangle: Swakopmund, Windhoek and Omaruru.

A second brewery opened its doors in 1912: the Kronenbrauerei (also written as Kronen-Brauerei) was the successor of the Swakopmunder Brauerei, indicating that the Swakopmunder Brauerei was out of business[52] Johann Heuschneider was the director of the Kronenbrauerei, an interesting man who would become a key figure in the history of the brewing industry of Namibia.[53] The brewery was located in the middle of town and was famous for its Kronenbrau, its main brand of beer. The water in Swakopmund had an excessively high saline content, it was after all a harbour town. Therefore, the water needed to be distilled before it could be used for the production of beer.[54] This may very well

---

& Co." More research is needed to see how this fits into the story. NSS, Fitzner, R., Adressbuch für Deutsch-Südwestafrika 1908 (Berlin 1908) 16, 83.

[52] SSS, Gründung der ersten Brauerei; this is also mentioned in NSS, Jahresbericht der Windhuker Handelskammer 1912; NAN, F002-cp, H. Heuschneider, Kleine Chronik der Hansa-Brauerei 2005 3; SSS, 2004.19.33, Gründung der ersten Brauerei 1912, Felsenkeller-Brauerei in Windhoek.

[53] Johann Heuschneider was not only involved in the Kronenbrauerei, but also in the Felsenkellerbrauerei, Union Brewery and Hansa Brewery. All of these breweries are discussed in this book.

[54] SSS, 2000.1.907, Erweiterung der Kronen-Brauerei.

Fig. 8: Advertisement for Rudolph Jauch's brewery, 1901.

have resulted in extra costs but was necessary to make the beer suitable for consumption. In 1914, Heuschneider and his company are mentioned in an overview of companies in Swakopmund.[55]

The business of the Kronenbrauerei grew rapidly, proving that its brew was widely popular. A newspaper article from 1913 discusses the expansion of the Kronenbrauerei in Swakopmund. The brewing industry at the time was growing, and locally produced beers displaced almost entirely the imported German beers via steamers. The company of Heuschneider made a couple of significant enlargements to the brewery. A new boiler house was built, the ice plant was enlarged, and the fermentation and storage cellars were extended as well.[56] A few years later, in 1919, the company was able to build a brewery deep in the heart of 'enemy territory': Windhoek, the place of its main competitor.[57] The brewers of Swakopmund had certainly left their mark on the brewing industry of GSWA.[58]

---

[55] H. Rautenberg, *Das alte Swakopmund: 1892–1919* (Swakopmund 1967) 324.
[56] SSS, 2000.1.907, Erweiterung der Kronen-Brauerei.
[57] SSS, 2004.31.28, Zur Feier der Eröffnung der Kronen-Brauerei in Windhoek.
[58] The building of the Kronenbrauerei in Swakopmund was later turned into the Grapevine Restaurant: NAN, F002-cp, H. Heuschneider, Kleine Chronik der Hansa-Brauerei 2005 3. Currently the place is transformed into the Swakopmund Plaza. Some of the remnants of the old brewery became visible during the construction work of the Plaza, but everything is now turned into modern glass and cement.

Fig. 9: The Kronenbrauerei originated in Swakopmund. This is their brewery in Windhoek, that opened in 1919.

Windhoek: The Centre

Windhoek was the centre of all brewing activity in Namibia. The city owes its existence to a few hot springs.[59] The Nama named the place |A||gams, which means "hot water" or "fire water." The Herero named it *Otjomuise*, meaning "place of the smoke." The changing of the name to Windhoek in itself is surrounded by smoke. The main theory is that Jonker Afrikaner named the settlement after the Winterhoek Mountains that were near the birthplace of his father, Jager Afrikaner.[60] In fact, Windhoek had many different names in the past, as Gunter von Schumann eloquently shows.[61] In the early 1900s, two breweries emerged in Windhoek: the Schmidt Brauerei in Klein Windhoek and the Felsenkellerbrauerei in the centre of town. Both companies merged in 1912 but will first be discussed individually below.

What happened with the buildings of the Swakopmunder Brauerei and the Kronenbrauerei in Windhoek is not clear.

[59] For more information regarding the history of Windhoek, see B. Bravenboer, *Windhoek: Capital of Namibia* (Windhoek 2004); C. von Dewitz, *Windhoek: A brief city guide* (Windhoek 2009).

[60] A.P.J. Albertyn, *Die Ensiklopedie Van Name In Suidwes-Afrika* (Pretoria 1984) 101–102.

[61] For a more elaborate context on the name of Windhoek, see G. von Schumann, Windhoek: a place of many names in the past, NamPost, March 1995, 22–23.

In Klein Windhoek, a brewery was opened by Friedrich Schmidt in 1902.[62] His story shows the remarkable trajectories people can have in a lifetime. Schmidt was born in 1867 in Nähermemmingen, a small village in Germany, as a son of a brewer. In search of adventure, he made the long journey to Africa and arrived in Swakopmund in the year 1901. Schmidt travelled further into the interior of the Protectorate and a year later he established a brewery in Klein Windhoek. His story came to light through his granddaughter Brigitte Schünemann and her family, who have a wonderful collection of photos, newspaper articles and other documents, and were kind enough to share these documents with me.

One particular photo shows the crew of the Klein Windhoek brewery and a banner with "Article 11 Schmidt Bier" written on it. Article 11 of the company's Articles of Association meant that whenever Mr. Schmidt was in town, the beer was free of charge for his employees. Needless to say, Schmidt had happy co-workers. A few years later, he stopped working as a brewer due to health reasons: Schmidt was no longer allowed to drink alcohol and therefore saw no use in being a brewer who cannot drink.[63]

A second brewery opened up in the centre of town. The Felsenkellerbrauerei was founded in 1902 by Karl Bauer and Richard Kretschmann.[64] The brewery was located on the intersection of Tal Street and Garten Street – the building still stands proud today in contemporary Windhoek. At that time, clear water flowed through the Tal Valley.[65] Bauer and Kretschmann bought a piece of land from the government on the 17th April 1902 and are named in the documents as brewery owners and brewers.[66] On the 28th October 1902, Bauer already sent a letter with "Felsenkeller-Brauerei Windhoek" written on the letterhead.[67] A big change in the company's structure occurred five years later, in 1907. In that year Kretschmann became the sole owner of the land.[68] Subsequently, a contract

---

[62] Although the South West Africa Annual mentions the name of Heinrich, the correct name is actually Friedrich, according to his granddaughter. NSS, South West Africa Annual, 1953 / Suidwes-Afrika-Jaarboek, 1953; Interview with Brigitte Schünemann, 4th February 2016.

[63] Interview with Brigitte Schünemann, 4th February 2016. Brigitte Schünemann, together with a number of family members, showed me several photos, beer mugs, news articles, and a brewing diploma of Schmidt, and told me many stories about his life. My interview was primarily conducted with Brigitte Schünemann. After Schmidt stopped working as a brewer, a heavy influenza killed many brewers in the territory in 1918. This caused Schmidt to come back to the brewery every day to supervise the brewing procedures. He used one of the first motor cars in the country. After forty years of living and working in South West Africa, Schmidt returned to Germany, where he died and is buried.

[64] C. von Dewitz, *Windhoek: A brief city guide* (Windhoek 2009) 50–51.

[65] NSS, South West Africa Annual, 1953.

[66] NAN, BWI 184, Grunderwerb. Felsenkeller Brauerei (Vormals Karl Bauer und Kretzschmann): Verhandelt, 17/06/1903. While the file name says "Kretzschmann," the documents in the file say Kretschmann. The latter version is used in this book.

[67] NAN, BWI 184, Grunderwerb. Felsenkeller Brauerei (Vormals Karl Bauer und Kretzschmann).

[68] NAN, BWI 184, Grunderwerb. Felsenkeller Brauerei (Vormals Karl Bauer und Kretzschmann): Gou-

Fig. 10: A postcard from the Schmidt Brauerei in Klein Windhoek.

from 1907 shows the establishment of the Felsenkellerbrauerei G.m.b.H. Kretschmann is named as brewery-owner and Johann Heuschneider, the same man who founded the Kronenbrauerei, is named as the master brewer.[69] Bauer is nowhere to be found in the contract. Presumably, he stepped out of the brewing business.

These changes in the company's structure and leadership may sound insignificant, but the involvement of Heuschneider is actually a big deal, because he was an influential person in Namibia's beer history. Not only did he start the Kronenbrauerei in Swakopmund, he also founded the Union Brewery and the better known Hansa Brewery (which produced the famous Tafel Lager). The records from this research show, however, that before this whole saga began, Heuschneider worked for a number of years in the Felsenkellerbrauerei. Why Heuschneider eventually left is unclear, but he spent the remainder of his career starting rival businesses.

With the formation of the new company structure in 1907, a number of personal changes followed. Two days after the signing of the treaty, Kretschmann began selling his shares. This also continued in 1908.[70] Documents from 1910 indicate that he left

---

vernementssekretär in Windhoek, 10/01/1908, to the Kaiserliche Bezirksamt.

[69] NAN, HRW 9, Handelsregistersache. Felsenkellerbrauerei Windhuk: Gesellschaftsvertrag 10/07/07; SSS, 2004.19.33, Gründung der ersten Brauerei 1912, Felsenkeller-Brauerei in Windhoek; NSS, Fitzner, R., Adressbuch für Deutsch-Südwestafrika 1908 (Berlin 1908) 18.

[70] NAN, HRW 9, Handelsregistersache. Felsenkellerbrauerei Windhuk: several documents show the selling of shares. They are all present in this file.

Fig. 11: The interior of the Schmidt Brauerei in Klein Windhoek.

GSWA and moved to Canada.[71] In the meantime the public was informed about the new company via publications in the Deutsch-Südwestafrikanischen Zeitung and the Windhuker Nachrichten on the 15th October 1907. The leaders of the company were named as master brewer Heuschneider and director Franz Gramowski.[72] But as suggested above, Heuschneider was not involved in the company for long. Only three years later, in June 1910, Leopold Mahler became the new director of the company.[73] A few months thereafter, in November, Heuschneider was replaced as a master brewer by a man named Fritz Hummel.[74] The reasoning behind this decision is unclear, but a conflict was born, as the remainder of this chapter shows.

For a few years, the two breweries in Klein Windhoek and in the centre of town managed to brew and market their beers for the public. They produced Helles Bier (a Pilsener type of lager) and Dunkles Bier (a Munich type of lager). Seasonally, a Bockbier was produced. Draught beer was also present in Windhoek and throughout the territory.[75] The

---

[71] NAN, HRW 9, Handelsregistersache. Felsenkellerbrauerei Windhuk: Ausfertigung 06/12/1910, and other documents present in this file.
[72] NAN, HRW 9, Handelsregistersache. Felsenkellerbrauerei Windhuk: Bekanntmachung 15/10/1907.
[73] NAN, HRW 9, Handelsregistersache. Felsenkellerbrauerei Windhuk: Bekanntmachung 17/06/1910.
[74] NAN, HRW 9, Handelsregistersache. Felsenkellerbrauerei Windhuk: Bekanntmachung 03/11/1010.
[75] Ibid.

Fig. 12: Felsenkellerbrauerei in Tal Street, Windhoek.

young brewing industry saw an increase in sales in 1910, partly because the construction of the railway through Windhoek resulted in an increase of thirsty domestic customers.

Nonetheless, competition of imported beers from Germany remained fierce and thus the future of the developing local brewing industry was uncertain. Substituting imported beers for locally brewed products was a slow and uneven process. In 1911, the Chamber of Commerce in Windhoek recognised the difficulties the small breweries were facing and pointed out that support from the government was desirable in order to keep the fledgling industry alive.[76]

The next year brought no improvement. In time, the newly constructed railway actually reduced the profit margin for beer brewers and unfavourable new government regulations made it more difficult to serve beer.[77] The growing shortage of money and high freight costs troubled the Felsenkellerbrauerei in Windhoek.[78] Under difficult circumstances, the brewers worked hard and managed to achieve small successes. Slowly, the beer imports from Germany decreased significantly and the local breweries were able

---

[76] NSS, Jahresbericht der Windhuker Handelskammer, 1910–1911 11–22.
[77] NSS, Jahresbericht der Windhuker Handelskammer, 1911–1912 12. NAN, F002-JX/0195, Bericht der Felsenkeller Brauerei Aktiengesellschaft 1912.
[78] NSS, Jahresbericht der Windhuker Handelskammer 1912 17–18.

to conquer the market. Breweries even bought or leased hotels in order to reach a larger group of customers. The profit margin of beer remained very low, due to the high rail tariffs, and thus remained an obstacle for the expansion of the industry.[79] All in all, it proved to be troublesome for these daring brewers and their companions to keep their businesses going.

As a result of the challenging economic circumstances, the companies from Klein Windhoek and the centre of town finally merged in 1912, forming the Felsenkellerbrauerei A.G. On the 10th February 1912, a group of businessmen met in the Hotel zur Kaiserkrone, where it was decided that the two breweries should be merged.[80] Six days later, the Felsenkellerbrauerei A.G. was founded and the two independent breweries in Windhoek became one.[81] A salient detail of the agreement between the two companies demonstrated how the businessmen feared the prospect of more competition in an already highly competitive industry. Friedrich Schmidt, the former owner of the brewery in Klein Windhoek, was explicitly forbidden to start another brewery in GSWA, with a possible fine of DEM 50,000 if he breached contract. This ensured that the remaining, unified brewery had most of the Windhoek market for itself.

The directors of the new company were the same people as the directors of the Felsenkellerbraurei, namely Mahler and Hummel. Otto Berger was named as the chairman of the Board of Inspection.[82] In the same year, a new brewhouse, beer hall and office were built for the Felsenkellerbrauerei, which shows us that the merger brought several advantages: the companies were able to join forces, maximize efficiency and expand their business. The construction company responsible for the construction work was Koch und Schultheiss. After the completion, the brewery in the centre of town was the largest industrial site in the colony.[83] The Felsenkellerei flourished despite the difficult economic circumstances and even managed to acquire a brewery in Omaruru, thereby dominating most of the interior of the Protectorate.[84]

---

[79] NSS, Jahresbericht der Windhuker Handelskammer 1913 21.
[80] NAN, BWI 428 Getränkeanmeldungen der Felsenkellerbrauerei: Mahler und Hummel, 12/06/1911, to the Kaiserliches Bezirksamt in Windhoek; NAN, HRW 10, Handelsregistersache. Felsenkellerbrauerei: Ausfertigung 10/02/1912.
[81] NAN, HRW 10, Handelsregistersache. Felsenkellerbrauerei: various documents. Also shown on the new letterhead are the words: "Felsenkeller-Brauerei Aktiengesellschaft — Windhuk. — Brauereien in Windhuk und Klein-Windhuk". NAN, BWI 428 Getränkeanmeldungen der Felsenkellerbrauerei: Mahler and Hummel in Windhoek, 11/04/1913, to the Kaiserliche Bezirksamt; NAN, HRW 10, Handelsregistersache. Felsenkellerbrauerei: Statut der Felsenkellerbrauerei Aktiengesellschaft 16/02/1912.
[82] NAN, F002-JX/0195, Bericht der Felsenkeller Brauerei Aktiengesellschaft 1912; SSS, 2000.1.861, Bericht der Felsenkellerbrauerei Aktiengesellschaft 1914/1915.
[83] NSS, Peters, W., *Baukunst in Südwestafrika 1884–1914* (Windhoek 1981) 190–191.
[84] NAN, HRW 10, Handelsregistersache. Felsenkellerbrauerei: year reports from 1910/11, 1911/12, 1913/14; NAN, MOK 1/2/1, Felsenkellerbrauerei, Parzelle 36, Blatt 5: various letters; NAN, MOK

Omaruru: The Mystery

Omaruru completes the beer triangle with a mysterious brewing history.[85] Omaruru is located at the Omaruru River and is an Otjiherero word for "bitter."[86] The bitter bush (*Pechuelloeschea leubnitziae*) grows in and around the town, and when animals eat the plant, their milk and meat becomes bitter.[87] Omaruru is a curious case: the available archival sources mention a brewery in this town, but at the same time it remains unclear how this company was founded or what eventually became of it.[88] Unlike the companies in Swakopmund and Windhoek, annual reports are non-existent and archival documents are scarce. How can we know what happened with this brewery? Carefully combining sources from three archives, oral histories, newspaper advertisements and a wooden beer mug that was found by accident makes it possible to shine a light on the mysterious Omaruru Brewery.

The story begins in 1907 when the Damara und Namaqua Handels-Gesellschaft, a trading company, bought the piece of land where the brewery was ultimately located.[89] Three years later, in 1910, a man called Daniel Bauer became the owner of the land. What happened in the meantime is unclear, but Bauer (a former farmer) bought the land from a certain Paul Canitz, who was by then the owner.[90] The plot was already in use: the fairly well-known Bahnhofshotel was located on it.[91] Bauer was unfortunately not a very successful hotelier. Already a year later, in 1911, he was indebted to the government and was

---

1/2/1, Felsenkellerbrauerei, Parzelle 36, Blatt 5. Dr. Fritzsche in Windhoek, 23/02/1921, to the Town Clerk of Okahandja; NLN, 96/0511 B, Namibia Breweries Limited, 1920–1995.

[85] For more on the history of Omaruru, see SSS, Pesch, L. and G. Murray, Omaruru: Im Laufe der Zeit (no publishing information); A. Otto and G. von Schumann, Hoofstraat Omaruru (unpublished, 1986).

[86] SSS, Pesch, L. and G. Murray, Omaruru: Im Laufe der Zeit (no publishing information) 2; I. Rudner and J. Rudner, *Axel Wilhelm Eriksson of Hereroland (1846–1901): His Life and Letters* (Windhoek 2006) 60.

[87] A.P.J. Albertyn, *Die Ensiklopedie Van Name In Suidwes-Afrika* (Pretoria 1984) 68.

[88] Various address books mention the existence of a brewery prior to the one that is discussed here. More research is necessary to find out what exactly happened. The earliest source that was found during the research for this book was from 1908, with the Weissbierbrauerei from J. Michalla. See NSS, Fitzner, R., Adressbuch für Deutsch-Südwestafrika 1908 (Berlin 1908) 69.

[89] NAN, Grundstück Omaruru. Parzelle 11 Blatt 3. Besitzer Bauer (Felsenkellerbrauerei Windhoek): contract with the Damara and Namaqua Handels-Gesellschaft, 1907.

[90] It is uncertain if this is the famous painter George Paul Canitz. Born in 1874 in Leipzig, Germany, Canitz was sent to live in GSWA for health reasons. According to his doctor, he needed the dry climate of GSWA. Canitz arrived in the territory in 1909 and this would coincide perfectly with the sale of the land in Omaruru. In 1925 he settled down at a farm near Stellenbosch, South Africa. He ran his own art school and taught at the University of Stellenbosch. Canitz died in 1959.

[91] NAN, Grundstück Omaruru. Parzelle 11 Blatt 3. Besitzer Bauer (Felsenkellerbrauerei Windhoek): Kaiserlicher Bezirksrichter in Omaruru, 10/12/1910, to the Kaiserlichen Gouverneur in Windhoek and the Kaiserliche Distriktsamt in Omaruru.

forced to sell the land.⁹² Three years later, in 1914, the plot came into the ownership of Mahler, the director of the Felsenkellerbrauerei. The clever businessman immediately sold the land to the Felsenkellerbrauerei.⁹³

The directors of the Felsenkellerbrauerei A.G. had plans to expand their business and desired to open up a brewery in Omaruru. The company bought two adjacent pieces of land and the brewery was finally erected in 1917.⁹⁴ The director was Conrad Piehl.⁹⁵ Mahler and Hummel sent a letter to the Secretary for the Protectorate in Windhoek on the 6th February 1918. They wrote that in a recent meeting between the directors, it was decided to erect a brewery at Omaruru, "for the purpose of supplying beer to our customers in the northern portion of the Protectorate."⁹⁶ This suggests that business was good and that the brewers had plans to export beer to the more northern part of GSWA. Mahler returned to Windhoek after a visit to Omaruru, where he had spoken with the Military Magistrate Major O'Reilly, who was in favour of the plans.⁹⁷ The site was already secured — only a brewing license was needed.⁹⁸

It did not take long before the brewing could commence. Mahler sent a letter to the Military Magistrate in Omaruru with an application for a license to brew and sell beer. On the 16th December 1918 the director wrote that his brewery would start with the

---

[92] NAN, Grundstück Omaruru. Parzelle 11 Blatt 3. Besitzer Bauer (Felsenkellerbrauerei Windhoek): Kaiserliches Distriktsamt in Omaruru, 20/09/1911; Gerichtsschreiber der Kaiserlichen Bezirksgerichts in Omaruru, 12/10/1912.

[93] NAN, Grundstück Omaruru. Parzelle 11 Blatt 3. Besitzer Bauer (Felsenkellerbrauerei Windhoek): 4. April 1913; A book on the history of Omaruru supports this claim but mentions a different year. Archival records show however the year is 1913. A. Otto and G. von Schumann, Hoofstraat Omaruru (unpublished, 1986) 35.

[94] A. Otto and G. von Schumann, Hoofstraat Omaruru (unpublished, 1986) 35; SSS, Pesch, L. and G. Murray, Omaruru: Im Laufe der Zeit (no publishing information) 15. According to Von Schumann, the hotel was demolished. But in the letters from 1920 it becomes clear that the hotel is still in use during the war. NAN, ADM 244, Claims: Felsenkeller Brauerei: Mahler in Windhoek, 10/02/1920, to the Secretary of the Protectorate of S.W.A.

[95] A. Otto and G. von Schumann, Hoofstraat Omaruru (unpublished, 1986) 35. The directory (Südwestafrikanisches Adressenbuch) of 1921–1922 mentions the existence of a brewery in Omaruru. Specifically, the Felsenkeller-Brauerei A.-G. is named, with C. Piehl as the director, see NSS, Südwestafrikanisches Adressenbuch 1921.22 / Directory of South West Africa 348.

[96] NAN, ADM 127, Breweries: Felsenkeller Brauerei establishment of a brewery at Omaruru: Mahler and Hummel in Windhoek, 06/02/1918, to the Secretary for the Protectorate.

[97] O'Reilly was the author of the Blue Book. When the German army was defeated the colony was governed under South African military rule. The Blue Book, the official title of which is "Report on the Natives of South-West Africa and Their Treatment by Germany," was a detailed report of the German occupation of Namibia, including the horrible atrocities that happened during the genocide of the Namibian War between 1904–1908. It was originally published in January 1918. J. Silvester and J.B. Gewald (eds.), *Words Cannot Be Found. German Colonial Rule in Namibia: An Annotated Report of the 1918 Blue Book* (Leiden 2003).

[98] NAN, ADM 127, Breweries: Felsenkeller Brauerei establishment of a brewery at Omaruru: Mahler and Hummel in Windhoek, 06/02/1918, to the Secretary for the Protectorate.

Fig. 13: The crew from the brewery at Omaruru.

work on the 1ˢᵗ January 1919. The letterhead on the paper already mentioned the existence of an entity in Omaruru: "Felsenkellerbrauerei Aktien Gesellschaft Windhuk — Omaruru".[99] The Secretary for the Protectorate in Windhoek, D.F. Herbst, sent a letter to the Military Magistrate on the 28ᵗʰ December 1918, stating that the issue of the license was approved.[100]

Little is known about the few years that the company was functioning in Omaruru. A beautiful undated picture from the private collection of Gunter von Schumann shows the first crew of the brewery. We see a group of around twenty people sitting and standing around five enormous beer barrels, some of them have a bottle or mug of beer in their hand. The brand name "Omaruru Urquell" is written on the wooden barrels.[101] The beer

---

[99] NAN, ADM 127, Breweries: Felsenkeller Brauerei establishment of a brewery at Omaruru: Mahler in Omaruru 16/12/1918, to the Military Magistrate Mayor O'Reilly Esqu.

[100] NAN, ADM 127, Breweries: Felsenkeller Brauerei establishment of a brewery at Omaruru: D.F. Herbst, 28/12/1919 in Windhoek, to the Military Magistrate in Omaruru.

[101] An original picture is located in the private collection of Gunter von Schumann. The same picture is located on the wall of the Brauhaus in Swakopmund. According to the owner of the Brauhaus, it was gifted by a family member of one of the former employees. Unfortunately, he does not know anything else about its history. The picture is also to be found in SSS, Pesch, L. and G. Murray, Omaruru: Im Laufe der Zeit (no publishing information) 15. In Windhoek, the brand Windhoek Urquell was produced, as newspaper advertisements from around this period show.

Figure 14: The wooden cup from the brewery in Omaruru.

produced by the Omaruru brewery was popular.[102] I found one of the rare pieces of evidence of the brewery by accident, whilst drinking a beer in the contemporary Brauhaus in Swakopmund, a German-style bar. Among the many ornaments that were on display in the bar was a wooden beer mug, with the inscription "Omaruruer Urquell."[103] It is a tangible reminder of the era during which Omaruru had a brewery.

The general economic depression in SWA from around the 1920s resulted in a decline in the consumption of beer, and therefore the plant was closed by the South West Breweries (the successor of the Felsenkellerbrauerei) in 1920. The brewery was later used as a tannery, then as an engineer shop and is currently used as a hall for music performances and other functions. According to another source, the reason for the closure was the mass deportation of Germans after the First World War. Germans formed the main customers market for the brewery. Omaruru as a whole suffered from the decision to close the plant as well as other economic misfortunes. Fear grew that the town would become deserted. The black and white photo of the crew, the wooden mug and newspaper advertisement are the only visual artefacts that keep the memory of the brewery alive.[104]

---

[102] Ibid.
[103] Why the beer brand is spelled slightly differently compared to the barrels on the photo is not clear.
[104] A. Otto and G. von Schumann, Hoofstraat Omaruru (unpublished, 1986) 35; conversation with Gunter von Schumann on the 29th October 2015. The NSS Annual Report notes that the brewery was closed down between 1920–1922, see NSS, Annual Report, 17–18; NSS, Annual Report of the Windhoek Chamber of Commerce, 29th November 1920 – 31st March 1922 17f; SSS, Pesch, L. and

The Great War

In 1914, GSWA was invaded by South African forces as a result of the First World War.[105] Great Britain declared war on Germany on the 4th August 1914, and, through General Louis Botha, the Union of South Africa offered help. In a telegram, the General and Prime Minister stated that the government of South Africa was willing to deploy the Union Defence Force for the performance of the tasks entrusted to the Imperial Troops. Great Britain's satisfactory response led quickly to an invasion of GSWA.[106] The war impacted the brewing business in the country in several ways and proved to be a real 'game changer' for the brewing events that followed thereafter. These reasons will be discussed below.

Firstly, the breweries were affected by a problematic import of ingredients, equipment and other goods. Normally, the companies would import the brewing ingredients such as hops and malt from Germany and other foreign countries, but the war hampered these endeavours. The businesses in the African territory also suffered from the ongoing fighting and political uncertainty.[107] Tough times were ahead.

Secondly, some of the breweries' properties were taken over by foreign troops. The Felsenkellerbrauerei leased for instance the Hohenzollern Hotel in Usakos to an August Ebrecht for a period of five years.[108] At that time, it was normal that breweries and hotels worked closely together. But as a result of the war, the Imperial Troops occupied Usakos and the hotel was used for military purposes. The brewers could not execute their intended plans for the hotel. Given the worsening economic circumstances, this was a disaster for the young brewing company. Records show that the directors made an attempt to recover some of the costs. In a letter from the 26th October 1915, Mahler and Hummel asked the Commandant of the Union Forces in Usakos to pay a suitable rent.[109] Thus they hoped to be compensated for their losses. If the rent was ever paid is unknown.

G. Murray, Omaruru: Im Laufe der Zeit (no publishing information) 15; NSS, Annual Report of the Windhoek Chamber of Commerce, 29th November 1920 – 31st March 1922 28; Interview with Gunter von Schumann, 18th February 2016.

[105] See G. L'ange, *Urgent Imperial Service: South African Forces in German South West Africa 1914–1915* (Cape Town 1991); G. McGregor and M. Goldbeck, *The First World War in Namibia: August 1914 – July 1915* (Windhoek 2014).

[106] Ibid., 12.

[107] NAN, F002-JX/0195, Bericht der Felsenkeller Brauerei Aktiengesellschaft 1912; SSS, 2000.1.861, Bericht der Felsenkellerbrauerei Aktiengesellschaft: 1914/1915, 1915/1916, 1916/1917 (three editions are present in this file).

[108] NAN, ADM 244, Claims: Felsenkeller Brauerei: Agreement of lease.

[109] NAN, ADM 244, Claims: Felsenkeller Brauerei: Mahler and Hummel in Windhoek, 26/10/1915, to the Commandant of the Union Forces in Usakos. Several letters followed, all in this file.

Thirdly, even the brewery's possessions were sometimes stolen by foreign forces. Again, the brewery from Windhoek was in trouble. In early 1914, the Felsenkellerei received 1020 new bags for the transport of malt to and from Europe from their agents in Hamburg, Germany. The bags were stored in the brewery complex in Windhoek when the Union Troops arrived but were stolen on the 24th June 1915 by a unit of the very same Troops. Hummel wrote a claim to the Secretary of the Protectorate.[110]

Furthermore, brewery properties were damaged by the actions of military troops. Two days after Hummel's letter (in which he asked to be compensated for the stolen malt bags) a fire broke out in the Bahnhofs-Hotel in Omaruru because of South African soldiers.[111] The hotel was located next to the brewery and belonged to the brewing company. The fire destroyed some of the furniture: six tables, three chairs, and more. Mahler filed a claim but the insurance company did not acknowledge obligation for compensation of the losses. As "an act of grace," they did pay for half of the ascertained amount of loss.[112] In another case, 40 sheets of second-hand corrugated iron for the same hotel were allegedly destroyed by military personnel and the brewery filed a claim with the government.[113] Even in 1924, years after the fighting had ended, the directors were occupied with handling the claimed "war losses" caused by the Union Troops.[114]

On the other hand, the South African soldiers enjoyed drinking very much. When the South African troops invaded Swakopmund, it only took them a few days to conquer the town. In order to make the town a stronghold against enemies, the soldiers fortified their surroundings with all the building material they could lay their hands on. After a while, a new regiment of soldiers arrived. Among them was a private who accidentally put the bayonet of his rifle in the newly built wall — only to find out that clear beer was flowing out of it. The new regiment of soldiers had not realized that their predecessors fortified the wall using beer kegs. A happy drinking party ensued and it did not take long before most of the kegs in the wall were empty, after which General Botha put an end to the drinking. This caused the soldiers to design a mock grave where they expressed their sorrow as they ritually buried a number of beer bottles.[115]

---

[110] NAN, ADM 244, Claims: Felsenkeller Brauerei: Hummel in Windhoek, 24/05/1916, to the Secretary of the Protectorate.

[111] NAN, ADM 217, Claims: Felsenkeller Brauerei: Boysen, Wneff (?) & Co. For Fire Insurance Magdeburg in Windhoek, 27/10/1920, to the Felsenkeller Brewery AG; Mahler in Windhoek, 10/02/1920, to the Secretary of the Protectorate S.W.A.

[112] Ibid.

[113] NAN, ADM 217, Claims: Felsenkeller Brauerei: Mahler in Windhoek, 10/02/1920, to the Secretary of the Protectorate S.W.A.

[114] NAN, ADM 244, Claims: Felsenkeller Brauerei: Atg. Secretary for South West Africa, 18/06/1924, to Dr. Franz in Windhoek.

[115] A similar story can be found in the magazine Flamingo (May 2012, by Ed Jenkins), but does not contain

The Great War was quickly over for the inhabitants of GSWA. Already in 1915, the German forces were defeated and the territory was occupied by South Africa. The formal act of surrender by the German troops was signed on the 9th July 1915.[116] The German control of the colony had come to its end — on the same day, the South African General Botha proclaimed martial law over the country.[117] An uncertain period of time commenced for everyone in the territory. Only time could tell what eventually would happen with the country.

The Beer War

When the Great War ended, the so-called Beer War began. From the numerous small breweries that popped up when the settler economy emerged in the early 1900s, only two companies were able to survive after the difficult war period. Those two companies dominated and divided the beer market. On the one hand there was the Kronenbrauerei in Swakopmund and Windhoek (led by Heuschneider), on the other hand there was the Felsenkellerbrauerei in Windhoek and Omaruru (led by Mahler). Both companies also obtained pieces of land for depots and hotels in other parts of the country. Heuschneider and Mahler must have been great rivals. Heuschneider was after all one of the founders of the Felsenkellerbrauerei but left when Mahler became the director. The rivalry between them resulted in what the newspapers described as a "Bierkrieg," a beer war.[118]

Both breweries aimed to increase their market share and (already before the war) undertook actions to expand their business operations. For instance, in 1913, the possible opening of an extension of the Kronenbrauerei in Windhoek "in the near future" was mentioned. The Kronenbrauerei came originally from Swakopmund and was embraced by the local community. Plans to build a brewing plant in the heart of Windhoek, where its main competitor was located, was nothing but a bold move.

Heuschneider launched a public attack on the "unpleasant characteristics" of the Windhoek water used by the Felsenkellerbrauerei in a local newspaper, to persuade customers to drink his beer. According to the message in the newspaper, the brewers from Swakopmund wanted to "bring a defeat" to Windhoek by offering fresh "Fassbier" (draft

---

    sources. I contacted Mr. Jenkins, who was so kind to send me a list of his sources. I could thus confirm the story. See: G. L'ange, *Urgent Imperial Service: South African Forces in German South West Africa 1914–1915* (Cape Town 1991). I would like to thank Mr. Jenkins for his help.

[116] M. Wallace, *A History of Namibia: From the Beginning to 1990* (Cape Town 2011) 205–206.
[117] G. McGregor and M. Goldbeck, *The First World War in Namibia: August 1914 – July 1915* (Windhoek 2014) 62.
[118] SSS, 2000.1.1013, Der Bierkrieg 1916.

beer) and "Flaschenbier" (bottled beer) to all customers.[119] The Felsenkellerei on the other hand was also full of ambitions for the future. Several building plans from the post-war period show the many extensions of their brewery, allowing for a better and larger production of beer.[120]

What followed was a heated debate that took place in the newspaper that became today's Allgemeine Zeitung. Both Heuschneider and the directors of the Felsenkellerbrauerei published open letters in which they continued to criticise each other. Take, for example, the Kronenbrauerei's publication of a special newspaper insert full of insults concerning their rivals from Windhoek on the 19th July 1916. Only three days later, on the 22nd July, the Felsenkellerbrauerei responded with its own newspaper insert, accusing Heuschneider of brewing his beer with seawater:

> Sie sind auch wahrscheinlich der einzige Brauer, welcher glaubt, aus Seewasser Bier machen zu können. Nun Ihnen aber keine Wissenschaft das schlechteste Wasser der Welt zum Bierbrauen geeignet Machen…[121]

On the 1st August, the Kronenbrauerei responded ferociously, and this rivalry went on and on. In 1919 the Kronenbrauerei finally opened a brewery in Windhoek, deep in the heart of enemy territory. The Felsenkellerei was after all founded in Windhoek. To celebrate this momentous occasion, a special Bierzeitung was published, a well known phenomenon in brewing cirlces. A Bierzeitung is as a satiric poem for a selected audience, in most cases employees, friends and families The poem for the opening of the Kronenbrauerei in Windhoek was nearly two meters long (!) and mocked Mahler and Müller, directors of the rivalling Felsenkellerbrauerei, and also made a little fun of their own boss, Heuschneider. Here is an excerpt from the Bierzeitung:

> Windhuker Morgensprache.
> Ein Gespräch zwi-chen zwei Handwerkern.
>
> Müller: Na, mein lieber Maler, Sie sind ja so verschnupft?
> Maler: Ja das kommt von dem verfluchten Heuschn-hatschi!
> Müller: Heuschn-eider Tausend!
> Maler: Dummes Zeug! Heuschn-upfen!!
> Müller: Ach nee! Hatschi – Prost.[122]

---

[119] SSS, 2000.1.907, Erweiterung der Kronen-Brauerei.
[120] NAN, ADM 120, Plans. Felsenkeller Brauerei. New Building; NAN, ADM 121, Plans. Felsenkeller Brauerei. New Building; NAN, ADM 122, Plans. Felsenkeller Brauerei. Shed; NAN, ADM 123, Building Plan. Felsenkeller Brewery. Tal Street. Additions: Beer Cooling Room. Plot 142/35 Section 4.
[121] SSS, 2000.1.1013, Der Bierkrieg 1916: 19th July 1916. The full original version can be found at the Namibia Scientific Society: NSS, Interimistische Zeitschrift für Übersetzungen (Von der Censur genehmigt.).
[122] SSS, 2004.31.28, Zur Feier der Eröffnung der Kronen-Brauerei in Windhoek.

Fig. 15: The Bierzeitung from the Kronenbrauerei, 1919.

The Formation of South West Breweries

The Beer War continued for a few years but was difficult to sustain due to the tedious economic circumstances and political uncertainty that followed the First World War. The rivalry between the Kronenbrauerei and Felsenkellerbrauerei only came to a conclusion when both companies were merged into South West Breweries (SWB) in 1920. The separate companies were struggling to maintain their brewing operations, symbolised by the fact that they had to raise the prices of their beer.[123] It is likely that the accumulating misfortunes in terms of economic headwind and political uncertainty resulted in a lack of perspective for both companies to remain active in the long term.

By that point in time, two young German bankers, Hermann Ohlthaver and Carl List, had entered the territory. In 1919, the ambitious, young men quickly founded the now famous company Ohlthaver & List Group and bought up the relatively small breweries in Swakopmund, Windhoek and Omaruru, taking advantage of the dire situation these

---

[123] NSS, Das Brennglas, No. 1, Jahrg. 1920; different documents from NBL explicitly say that the difficulties of the breweries were the reason why Ohlthaver and List bought them. One of the many examples: NLN, 96/0511 B, Namibia Breweries Limited, 1920–1995. This is also echoed in B. Bravenboer, *Windhoek: Capital of Namibia* (Windhoek 2004) 48–49.

companies were facing.[124] An anonymous author in *Das Brennglas*, a satirical magazine, described this historical event in the poem "Trinkt Felsenkeller! Trinkt Kronenbräu!":

> FELSENBIER! hieß es, das Bier für Ästheten,
> KRONENBIER aber: Getränk für Proleten.
> (…)
> Leo gab Johann den Bruderkuss
> und daraus entstand der Zusammenschluss.
> (…)
> Trotz wahrhaft enormen Hindernissen
> Die Brauereien sind zusammengeschmissen!
> FELSEN und KRONEN jetzt ist einerlei
> Beides Produkt des SÜDWEST-BRAUEREI.[125]

On the 29th October 1920, South West Breweries Limited (SWB) was officially founded. The Memorandum and Articles of Association specifically stated that the company took over the Kronenbrauerei and the Felsenkellerbrauerei, and that the individual breweries in Swakopmund, Windhoek and Omaruru were amalgamated. List was listed as one of the shareholders, but Ohlthaver was not.[126] SWB is the first brewery in the history of Namibia whose name is explicitly aligned with the political circumstances, as German South West Africa was changed into South West Africa following the defeat of the German troops. Two months later, on the 1st January 1921, South Africa began to rule SWA on the basis of a League of Nations mandate and the name of the territory and a new era began.

In conclusion, the emergence of the beer industry can largely be explained in terms of war. The brutal colonisation of GSWA made the settling of an increasing number of settlers possible. The settlers imported beer from Germany, but this practice became unsustainable due to the high costs, impractical organisation and taste preferences. In the early 1900s, a whole range of small breweries popped up all over the country. Their location can be explained through an analysis of the available population, water, and transport routes.

The First World War changed the brewing scene and pushed the territory into an economic depression and political uncertainty. Two companies survived: the Kronen-

---

[124] Since then Ohlthaver & List has grown to one of the most powerful and biggest business groups of Namibia, as it is active in the realms of brewing, real estate, farming, dairy, supermarkets, hotels, and more. Brenda Bravenboer is currently writing a company history, expected to be published in 2019 for the 100 year anniversary of O&L.

[125] NSS, Das Brennglas. Leo is Leopold Mahler, the director of the Felsenkellerbrauerei. Johann refers to Johann Heuschneider, the director of the Kronenbrauerei.

[126] NAN, F002-PA/0120, Memorandum and articles of the South West Breweries Limited 1920. Ohlthaver apparently left the country, although it remains uncertain why this was the case. The List family continued to dominate the brewery. Carl List remained the chairman until his son Werner List took over. Currently his grandson, Sven Thieme, is in a leading position.

brauerei (based in in Swakopmund and Windhoek) and the Felsenkellerbrauerei (based in Windhoek and Omaruru). After being fierce competitors, fighting each other in the so-called Beer War, the companies were merged by Ohlthaver & List, forming a single company called SWB. Decades later, SWB would transform into Namibia Breweries Limited (NBL), the brewing company that still exists today and has become synonymous with Namibia's beer industry But that is a story for the third chapter of this book. We now move on to the influence of South Africa on the developing beer market in SWA.

2 A Changing Beer Market, 1920–1970

The year 1920 marks in many ways the start of a new era in the development of the Namibian beer market. SWA was formally established as a mandate territory of the Union of South Africa. In the following years, a total of three new breweries emerged in the territory, and they immediately faced decades of difficulty: an economic depression, another worldwide war and a complicated and racial set of liquor laws were some of the obstacles the companies had to face. The brewers experienced lots of hardship but managed to keep their breweries open. The 1960s meant a huge break with past practices, as a number of historical events suddenly succeeded one another, forcing drastic changes in the beer industry. A lot can happen in a time period of fifty years, as this chapter will show.

Legal Consequences for Beer

The new political reality for (German) South West Africa had grave legal consequences for the making and drinking of beer. After the military campaign of South Africa had ended in 1915, South Africa occupied GSWA and military rule was established.[1] Five years later, the territory was declared a Class C Mandate territory by the League of Nations, the predecessor of the United Nations. The Union of South Africa became responsible for the mandate territory and simply named it South West Africa.

The Mandate Agreement was signed in Geneva on the 17th December 1920 and the martial law period ended formally on the 1st January 1921. At that moment, South Africa became the official mandatory power for SWA.[2] It may seem that this event is not relating to beer at all, but actually, alcohol formed an important part of the Mandate Agreement. Article 3 of the Mandate Agreement dealt exclusively with alcohol, and hence had a profound impact on the decades to come. Most importantly, the article declared that "The supply of intoxicating spirits and beverages to the natives shall be prohibited."[3] This was a measure to control the local population. Article 3 had far-reaching implications for brewers, customers, judges and politicians in the subsequent decades. Earlier legislation

---

[1] P. Hayes, J. Silvester, M. Wallace and W. Hartmann (eds.), *Namibia under South African Rule: Mobility and Containment 1915–46* (Oxford 1988) 22.
[2] M. Wallace, *A History of Namibia: From the Beginning to 1990* (2011 Cape Town) 206.
[3] NAN, JUS 156, Kaffir beer: Naturellesake: voorgestelde wysiging van drankwet om brou en drink van kafferbier deur naturelle op plase toe te laat; H. Siiskonen, 'Namibia and the Heritage of Colonial Alcohol Policy', *Nordic Journal of African Studies* Vol. 3 No. 1 (1994) 78.

already dealt with the sale of European beer to the African population.[4] Alcohol was an important trading item when the first contacts between Europeans and Africans were established, a time which the historian Harri Siiskonen described as "the wild decades of alcohol trade."[5]

The sale of alcohol to Africans was deliberated at the Brussels Conference in 1890 because increases in the supply of liquor made it more difficult to subject African communities to foreign rule.[6] Colonial authorities were concerned about an inebriated — and therefore unreliable — labour force. In addition, it was feared that alcohol can lead to disobedience. In GSWA, an ordinance dated 27th May 1895 regulated the retail and sale of spirituous liquors. Innkeepers and those who wanted to sell alcohol had to obtain a written license. Beer and other liquor could only be sold to the local population if they obtained written permission from the chief, local police or a doctor in case of sickness.[7]

Accordingly, legislative limitations for the African population to drink beer already existed prior to the Mandate Agreement. However, the fact that alcohol had such a prominent position in the Mandate Agreement showed the keen interest of the South African state in alcohol. The notorious Article 3 formed the starting point of a whole series of legislative efforts to control the local communities in this specific area of life.

The Liquor Licensing Proclamation of the 15th January 1920 gave a comprehensive legal framework for the intentions of the Mandate Agreement's third article. In many ways, the Proclamation was an elaboration of the Brussels Conference of 1890 and GSWA's ordinance of 1895, but it differed from it in two distinct ways. The practical effect of the previous legislation was limited because the colonial administration in the early years of colonisation had few resources to oppress the beer trade.[8] In 1920 however, the administration was better established than before: the capacities of the state increased and the control over the various ethnic groups that lived in the colony was severely strengthened. In addition, the South African government decided to actively use the beer market as a political instrument to control the population.

---

[4] Pan, L., *Alcohol in Colonial Africa* (Helsinki 1975).
[5] H. Siiskonen, 'Namibia and the Heritage of Colonial Alcohol Policy', *Nordic Journal of African Studies* Vol. 3 No. 1 (1994) 77–78.
[6] Ibid.
[7] WCARS, GH 1/460, Papers received from Secretary of State, London: general dispatches. The liquor traffic in the German Protectorate in South West Africa: M. Gosselin in Berlin, 05/09/1895, to Sir. E. Malet.
[8] Gordon, discussing the alcohol trade in the 1880, notes that "The Government was forced to act but their Verordnungs were rarely successfully or forcefully implemented." R. Gordon, Inside the Windhoek Lager: Liquor and Lust in Namibia, in: W. Jankowiak and D. Bradburd (eds.) *Drugs, labor, and colonial expansion* (Tucson 2003) 123.

Fig. 16: A zebra at work during the renovation of South West Breweries.

The Liquor Licensing Proclamation divided the beer market into two racial parts: the white population was allowed to drink, whereas the black population was not allowed to drink. It is an extraordinary document, one of the longest pieces of legislation of the South African era, that gives much insight in the minds of the colonial bureaucrats of that time. The Proclamation was largely based on the South African Liquor Act of 1928 (No. 30 of 1928).[9] The liquor law defined natives as "any person other than a European," an important definition that formed the basis for many forthcoming laws.

The sale of liquor to natives was prohibited — even if a local person had received liquor or had liquor in their possession, they were guilty of an offence. No liquor licenses were to be issued within the limits of native locations or reserves. Importing liquor into SWA became unlawful for the black population. The penalties for selling beer to an indigenous person were harsh and could add up to twelve months of imprisonment and hard labour.[10]

---

[9] NAN, F002-AA/1996, The liquor law of South-West Africa: being the Liquor Licensing Proclamation, 1920 (Proclamation no.6 of 1920), as amended from time to time, with notes, references to decided casses [sic] and other relevant legislation.

[10] NAN, F002-PA/0110, The liquor law of the South-West Africa Protectorate.

All in all, the new law was an ambitious, harsh and extensive document with far-reaching implications for both the African and the European communities. There was, however, one important loophole in this document, because it simply did not discuss the existence of home brewing. Logically, local communities kept on brewing their own beers, as they had been doing for centuries. In practice, two beer markets were created: one formal market for white colonial settlers and one informal market for the local population. Beer thus became a marker for racial identity and a place of contestation against the apartheid state.

Three New Breweries

Three new breweries emerged in the territory during the first years of the newly established SWA. The first company is SWB, founded in 1920 as a merger of several breweries. The first chapter dealt with this event in a more detailed manner. The fact that SWB was able to combine the strength of several smaller breweries meant that they instantly became the key player in the brewing industry. It is in this period of time that SWB on Tal Street (in the centre of Windhoek) expanded, under the technical leadership of one of its first managing master brewers, Julius Geier. The early days of the brewery is captured by an unusual black and white photograph of the construction site, showcasing a cart with several donkeys and one zebra.

The owner of the zebra was Julius Geier, a former master brewer at the Felsenkellerbrauerei.[11] Similar to the story of Friedrich Schmidt (from the Klein Windhoek brewery, discussed in Chapter One), the story of Julius Geier gives us a precious insight in the lives of European settlers of the territory. Geier was born in 1884 in Zwittau, in today's Czech Republic, where he received his initial training as a brewer in Pilsen at the famous Pilsen Brewery during 1903–1905. Subsequently, Geier underwent further practical training in the Löwen Brauerei in Dortmund, Germany. In 1911, he received his master brewer certificate in Berlin and travelled afterwards to SWA. In 1921, he married Ella Henker. On the 1st July 1928, Geier started his position as SWB's master brewer and his contract, still in possession of his family, is one of the rare historical artefacts of this period in brewing history.

Geier was thus placed in charge of the breweries in Windhoek and Swakopmund and was allowed to live on the brewing premises. The contract stated that Geier could not only live in the brewery free of charge, he would also receive free firewood, ice, and beer

---

[11] Geier's family shared the details of his life with me, I would like to thank Lothar Geier and Harald Geier for their kind assistance during my research.

Fig. 17: The exterior of the South West Breweries plant in Tal Street, Windhoek.

for his own consumption. Unfortunately, Geier passed away unexpectedly in 1935. His funeral happened to be a big event in Windhoek and many people showed up to pay their respects. All this bears witness to the prestige that was attached to being the leading master brewer of the largest brewery of the country at the time — something that is still the case today.[12]

The second company founded in the 1920s was the Union Brewery, which was officially founded in 1922 and was also located in Windhoek.[13] The company's name is probably a reference to the Union of South Africa, of which SWA was now a part. Before this research project commenced, the Union Brewery was almost completely forgotten. Its existence was discovered by accident during research conducted in the National Archives of Namibia, but unfortunately, not much information on the company is available. The Union

---

[12] Interview with Lothar Geier, 18th February 2016.
[13] SSS, 2004.19.33, Gründung der ersten Brauerei 1912, Felsenkeller-Brauerei in Windhoek: Hansa-Brauerei Limited in Swakopmund, 17/01/1929, to Ernst Sievert in Swakopmund; 50 Jahre Hansa-Brauerei Swakopmund, DHPS 19/01/1979; Daten zur Eröffnung der "Hansa Brauerei Ltd," am 19/01/1929; Hansa Brauerei Limited: 50th Anniversary Celebrations This Coming Weekend, Namib Times, 16/01/1979.

Brewery is mentioned a few times in various documents but only two small archival files actually contain any sort of information related to the company operations.[14] The company had GBP 8000 of capital, divided among four shareholders. The main shareholder was Ludwig Barella, who owned half of the shares. He is described as a retired businessman in the Memorandum of Association.

The big surprise lies in the other three shareholders, as they were members of the well-known Heuschneider family: Johann Heuschneider was the master brewer and his two sons, Hans and Paul, acted as engineers.[15] Heuschneider, as discussed, started his brewing career in the Felsenkellerbrauerei but had to leave after a few years. When he settled in Swakopmund, he founded the Felsenkeller's most important rival: the Kronenbrauerei. And now, only two years after these two companies merged, Heuschneider helped developing another business rival.

However, the Union Brewery was not a successful endeavour. The company was in business for only a short amount of time. Newspaper advertisements from April 1923 invited the public for the grand opening on the 1st May.[16] In July 1923, a year after the founding date, Hans and Paul Heuschneider allocated their shares to Barella, who now owned 7950 of the 8000 shares. The remaining 50 shares were owned by Johann Heuschneider, but he sent a letter to the Registrar of Deeds that he was leaving Windhoek and could no longer fulfil the duties of director. Barella was subsequently appointed as the new director.[17] The Heuschneider family travelled to Mozambique, and what happened with the brewery thereafter is uncertain. Five years later, in 1928, the company was deleted off the register and dissolved — in the same year as the Felsenkellerbrauerei, ironically enough.[18]

It is curious that the Heuschneider family left the existence of the Union Brewery out of their official family history. Heinz Heuschneider, the grandson of the famous Johann Heuschneider, wrote a published essay on his family's brewing history. In this document he describes how his family moved to Mozambique after they were done with the Kronenbrauerei in Swakopmund. However, he does not mention the Union Brewery

---

[14] The sources in the National Archives were incorrectly filed and were therefore not really accessible. I only found them with the help of the former director of the National Archives, Mr. Werner Hillebrecht. I am grateful for his help.

[15] The Memorandum of Association of the Union Brewery Limited was signed on the 4th July 1922. The Certificate of Incorporation (No. 17/1922) was signed on the 12th July 1922. The office was situated at Rehoboth Street, Old Limeworks, Erf 393/4, Windhoek, which was noted on the 4th October 1922. NAN, COM 17, The Union Brewery Limited (Private Company): Registrations.

[16] Advertisement from the Landes-Zeitung für Südwestafrika, 28th April 1923.

[17] NAN, COM 17, The Union Brewery Limited (Private Company): Returns.

[18] NAN, COM 17, The Union Brewery Limited (Private Company): Registrations: Notice No. 33 of 1928.

Fig. 18: An advertisement from the Union Brewery, 1923.

at all.[19] Ernst (Emil) Heuschneider, Heinz's brother, did the same in an interview with Brenda Bravenboer.[20] For now this seems to be the end of the line, it is unclear what happened with the Union Brewery. Perhaps yet undiscovered documents in archives or personal collections will illuminate this mystery.[21]

The third company that was founded at the dawn of South African occupation of the territory is the Hansa Brewery in Swakopmund, founded in the year 1928.[22] Hansa became the main competition to SWB and was — you may have guessed it — founded by a man named Johann Heuschneider. The company name refers to the Hanseatic League: also known as Hansa, the league was a confederation of guilds and towns in northern Europe, which dominated the regional trade in the middle ages. Sea navigation was an important aspect of this trade. Swakopmund was a harbour, similar to the important cities in the league. Moreover, the Heuschneider family had strong ties with the German city of Hamburg, one of the Hanseatic cities.[23]

Heuschneider and his family left Windhoek for Maputo in Mozambique to run a brewery but found it unpleasant to settle at the eastern coast of Africa.[24] They did not enjoy the climate in Mozambique and even contracted malaria. In those days, Swakopmund had a schnapps company that went out of business. Certain businessmen got hold of the premises and wanted to establish a brewery, in the spirit of the dissolved but still famous Kronenbrauerei. When the Heuschneider family got the chance to open up another brewery in SWA, they purchased machinery in Germany, transported it to the coastal town of Swakopmund and commenced with the brewing operations.[25]

---

[19] NAN, F002-cp, H. Heuschneider, Kleine Chronik der Hansa-Brauerei 2005.
[20] Interview Brenda Bravenboer with Ernst Heuschneider, 27th February 2012.
[21] One of the enigmas of the Union Brewery is Ludwig Barella, as it seems that he funded the brewing operation. The company files in the National Archives are not personally signed by Barella, but are signed by John Hugo Hill, in his capacity as holder of general power of attorney: NAN, COM 17, The Union Brewery Limited (Private Company): Registrations. This might indicate that Barella was not physically present in Windhoek during the signing of these documents. Today, there is a Barella House and Barella Street in Windhoek, indicating that Barella was an influential person. His obituaries appeared in the Allgemeine Zeitung on the 21st May 1951.
[22] The company was registered on the 30th November 1928, the business started on the 1st September 1928 and the first beer was ready on the 21st January 1929. SSS, Hansa-Brauerei Limited Swakopmund, 7. Geschäftsjahr 1935–1936 (uncatalogued).
[23] The brewing equipment of Hansa Brewery came for instance from Hamburg, they had an agent there and Heuschneider signed a document from Hamburg. Interview Brenda Bravenboer with Ernst Heuschneider, 27th February 2012; NAN, F002-NAMZ 0528, Andreas Vogt, Wine, beer and song in hotels of old Windhoek, Informanté, 2006 9; NAN, SWAA 3115, Monthly Revenue Returns: Alleged customs fraud Hansa Brewery Swakopmund: Sgd. J.W. Naude, Inspector. District Commandant, Omaruru, 24/02/1939, to The Commissioner, South West Africa Police; NAN, HRW 9, Handelsregistersache. Felsenkellerbrauerei Windhuk: Vollmacht, Johann Heuschneider, Hamburg, 30/06/1908.
[24] Interview Brenda Bravenboer with Ernst Heuschneider, 27th February 2012.
[25] NAN, F002-cp, H. Heuschneider, Kleine Chronik der Hansa-Brauerei 2005; SSS, 2004.19.33, Gründ-

Fig. 19: An employee of Hansa Brewery, Swakopmund.

Swakopmund finally had its own brewery again, and the old beer rivalry between Swakopmunders and people from Windhoek was restored in all its glory. 900 litres of beer and 400 sausages were consumed at the festive opening party of the Hansa brewery.[26] It truly was a family business: five members of the Heuschneider family were active in the brewery.[27] Hansa Brewery had depots all over SWA, but could also rely on a consumer base in South Africa. Depots were also located in some major South African towns: Cape Town, Johannesburg, Mossel Bay, Port Elizabeth, East London and Durban were among them.[28] In 1941, a new brewhouse was installed in Swakopmund, and further enlargements were implemented in 1946, such as new bottle washers, filling equipment, and storage tanks.

---

ung der ersten Brauerei 1912, Felsenkeller-Brauerei in Windhoek: several documents.

[26] SSS, 2004.9.17, Ein Teil Südwester Zeitgeschehens: Allgemeine Zeitung, 16th January 1979.

[27] Involved in the brewery were Johann, Emma, Hans, Paul, and Ernst Heuschneider, all holding various functions. SSS, Hansa-Brauerei Limited Swakopmund, 7. Geschäftsjahr 1935–1936 (uncatalogued); SSS, Hansa-Brauerei Limited Swakopmund, 8. Geschäftsjahr 1936–1937 (uncatalogued); SSS, Memorandum und Statuten der Hansa Brauerei Limited (uncatalogued).

[28] SSS, Hansa-Brauerei Limited Swakopmund, 7. Geschäftsjahr 1935–1936 (uncatalogued); SSS, Hansa-Brauerei Limited Swakopmund, 8. Geschäftsjahr 1936–1937 (uncatalogued); Interview Brenda Bravenboer with Ernst Heuschneider, 27th February 2012.

Fig. 20: The interior of the Hansa Brewery in Swakopmund.

These historical episodes prove that the brewing industry was developing in all sorts of ways; it truly was a lively scene with many aspects to it. Unfortunately, what followed thereafter were decades of difficulty for the bold brewers of SWA. In the 1930s, a raging global economic depression made it difficult for any business to survive. In the 1940s, the Second World War made it almost impossible to get raw materials from Europe. And in the 1950s, it became clear that the liquor law was highly problematic for both of the racially divided beer markets. These three main obstacles will be discussed below.

Economic Depression

The 1920s and 1930s were characterised by a severe economic depression. After the defeat of the German troops during WWI and the occupation of the territory by South Africa, the business climate became notoriously difficult. Many Germans had to leave the territory after the political change between 1915 and 1920, which was troublesome for the breweries because the German population constituted their main customer base. To

Fig. 21: A Windhoek Lager bottle in the SWB plant. This bottle shape was nicknamed "the hand grenade".

add to these problems, a drought and the "consequent dearth of capital impaired the purchasing power of the community," writes SWB in its financial report of 1924–1925. This was at a time when the brewery still had horses in its annual budget.[29] The situation was only aggravated by the worldwide economic depression that spread from the United States of America in the 1930s.

The brewers had trouble keeping their head above the water. The depression resulted in a "considerable reduction" in the consumption of beer, according to the Windhoek Chamber of Commerce. SWB had to close down the breweries in Omaruru and Swakopmund and focused its production on Tal Street in the centre of Windhoek. The

---

[29] NLN, South West Breweries Limited, Annual Report, 1924–1925.

premises in Windhoek were centrally located and were surrounded by a relatively larger consumer base than the other branches, which might explain why the Windhoek branch was saved. The Chamber of Commerce concludes its annual report with the statement that "the quality of the beers is excellent and […] superior to that of Union beers."[30] The brewers suffered from European competition. The ingredients for beer, bottles, and machinery doubled in price, while the excise duty had increased fourfold.[31]

The excise officer of SWA noted a "sharp decline in the production of beer" of SWB in July 1931, caused by the depression and the closing down of copper and diamond mines in Tsumeb and Lüderitz. SWB had to lay off employees and reduced the salaries of its personnel by 20%.[32] It is unsure how Hansa Brewery coped with the economic difficulties but we can be quite certain that the situation in Swakopmund was not any different from the rest of the country. Those tedious times were only aggravated in the years to come.

World War II

The Second World War impacted SWA, just as the First World War GSWA. There was, however, a noticeable difference between the character of both wars. During the First World War, foreign military forces rapidly occupied the area that is now Namibia. This did not occur during the Second World War, although the tension between the German and Afrikaner settler communities increased significantly, as the South African administration feared a German uprising. South Africa only 'acquired' SWA fairly recently and was afraid to lose it to an angry German community.

With the relatively large amount of German settlers in the territory and its already anxious stance against the South African government, the administration feared that this community would sympathise with fighting Germans abroad and would therefore take up arms. The impact of the Great War on GSWA is discussed in several history books — in contrast, the impact of WWII is in need of more research.[33] In contemporary Namibia, the best known story of the war is the seminal book *Wenn es Krieg gibt,*

---

[30] NSS, Annual Report of the Windhoek Chamber of Commerce, 29th November 1920 – 31st March 1922, 17–18.
[31] NSS, Report of Chamber of Commerce, Windhoek, 1923–1924, 8–9.
[32] NAN, SWAA 3113, Customs and Excise: Brewery Regulations: Excise officer in Windhoek, 17/11/1931, to the Secretary for South West Africa.
[33] Gordon writes that "A study on the Second World War in Namibia might be a fertile area of investigation" and already provides a number of ideas for this study. R. Gordon, 'The Impact of the Second World War on Namibia', *Journal of Southern African Studies* Vol. 19 No. 1 (1993) 147. Unfortunately, no significant research has been conducted on this topic ever since.

gehen wir in die Wüste by Henno Martin and Hermann Korn, the story of two Germans who moved into the desert when the war broke out.[34]

Less known is the story that the war also affected the breweries in SWA. The main problem for the breweries was the fact that they were no longer allowed to acquire raw material from Germany, because the South African government considered this as trading with the enemy.

The administration in Pretoria looked upon the breweries with great suspicion. At this time, two main breweries were active in the South West territory: SWB and Hansa Brewery. Both companies employed mainly Germans and were also actively engaged in international trade with partners in Germany. Most raw materials and machinery were acquired in Germany. The brewers were resourceful and quickly found other ways of acquiring the essential ingredients, brewing equipment, and other goods. For example, during the war years, SWB received hops from, among other countries, Yugoslavia, the United States, and Belgium.[35] Hansa Brewery imported ingredients and equipment from Denmark, the United States, Canada, Australia, and South Africa.[36]

The South African government secretly put a watch on the cables of both breweries and checked all of their correspondence with international trading partners for any suspicious behaviour.[37] The story of the intelligence reports (which were kept secret for a long time) reads like a detective novel. The intelligence reports confirmed that the Hansa Brewery was in contact with Siegfried and Hans Oppenheimer, two family members who travelled from Belgium to the United States in 1939. The two men started a business from a hotel room in New York and were believed to be one of the biggest global exporters of German hops since the war began. German hops was the desired brewing ingredient for

---

[34] M. Henno, *Wenn es Krieg gibt, gehen wir in die Wüste* (Windhoek 1970).
[35] It is remarkable how much effort was being put into transporting hops around the globe. Correspondence from 1940 with trading partners in London shows some of the difficulties encountered. It was not possible to ship hops from the Yugoslavian port Susak because the main route through the Adriatic Sea was cut off by Italy. An alternative plan was to rail the hops to Istanbul, and then ship them through the Suez Canal and the Red Sea to Cape Town. In Cape Town, the hops were to be put in wooden cases and brought to SWA. The government of South Africa, in the meantime, suspected those specific hops to come from Austria, which was regarded as enemy territory and therefore the trade would be a contravention of Regulation 8 (2) of Proclamation 201 of 1939, most probably a war measure preventing trade with Germany. NAN, SWAA 2569, Trading with the enemy. The South West Africa Breweries: The South West Breweries Limited in Windhoek, 23/08/1940, to the Secretary for South West Africa; Rosenfeld & Co. in London, 19/08/1940, to South West Breweries in Windhoek.
[36] NAN, SWAA 2572, Trading with the enemy. Hansa Breweries, Swakopmund: Max B. Gleassner in New York, 16/07/1941, to Hansa Brewery in Swakopmund; The Secretary for South West Africa in Windhoek, 30/09/1940, to the Secretary for Commerce and Industries in Pretoria.
[37] See countless of intelligence reports and copied cables in: NAN, SWAA 2572, Trading with the enemy. Hansa Breweries, Swakopmund; NAN, SWAA 2569, Trading with the enemy. The South West Africa Breweries. These files are a real treasure trove.

Fig. 22: A beer truck from South West Breweries.

breweries from all over the world, as it had a particular good quality and was produced in relatively large numbers When the war broke out, it became increasingly difficult to buy this precious ingredient.

The company of the Oppenheimers exported goods for a "Waffenexportfabrik," clearly not the name of a typical hops company, by putting goods on neutral Belgian ships in order to circumvent the laws against trading with Germany. The hops were given false certificates of origin and the traders used false names in their correspondence and papers. The Belgian trade route became impossible after a while. The Oppenheimers then used Leningrad as a new route, Istanbul and even the Trans-Siberian Railway where the Japanese government allegedly made an allocation of two million yen to facilitate the trade.[38] As a result of this information that was gathered by intelligence services, the authorities inspected a shipment and arms and ammunition for Germany were found. It was believed that "hops" was nothing but a mere code word for all sorts of illegal things. The intelligence reports, for example, mentioned that the Oppenheimers were also involved in the precious stone trade.[39]

This raised grave concerns for the Hansa Brewery, which, quoting a South African government official, "was looked upon with suspicion by the Union authorities because of

---

[38] NAN, SWAA 2572, Trading with the enemy. Hansa Breweries, Swakopmund; Secretary for Commerce and Industries, 09/04/1947, to the secretary for Commerce and Industry.

[39] Ibid.

its past activities."⁴⁰ The authorities most probably referred to an earlier series of "cleverly devised fraud" by the brewery management.⁴¹ Governments in Pretoria, Washington, and London worked together to investigate the concerns. In 1940, the SWA administration thoroughly inspected the books and records of the brewery. It was noted in the report that all 29 shareholders were "very strong Nazis."⁴² This was echoed in other confidential reports, and an investigation was instigated to find out the exact whereabouts of the Hansa shareholders.⁴³ The accusations constituted that the ownership of the brewery consisted of "various influential Nazis" and was buying illegal hops and other articles from German companies in Hungary or Slovakia.⁴⁴

Many Germans in SWA were put in internment camps during the war period.⁴⁵ Even in these camps, heavily guarded by South African police, people were able to brew in certain so-called "Geheimbrauereien." The prisoners managed to acquire sugar, raisins and grape juice, and went underground to secretly make the "*Gungai*," as they (nick)named the brew.⁴⁶ The stories of Hansa Brewery and the Geheimbrauereien in the internment

---

[40] Ibid. The same official wrote to the High Commissioner of the South Africa House in London that "Hansa Breweries have behaved in the past in a manner to justify their being regarded with grave suspicion in the Union." NAN, SWAA 2572, Trading with the enemy. Hansa Breweries, Swakopmund: Secretary for Commerce and Industries, day unknown, 11/1940, to the Secretary, office of the High Commissioner, South Africa House, London.

[41] Between 1932 and 1936, two managers, Joseph Sickel and Hans Willy Heuschneider, were accused of fraud by the South African authorities. The government compiled a detailed description of these charges. Sickel succeeded in bringing a golden chain and fur coat into the country without paying duty. In another instance, they would send a single shoe over the border (marked as "sample shoe"), and a week later the second shoe with a similar mark would turn up, in order to avoid duty. The inspector, Sgd. J.W. Naude, writes that "There is no doubt that politically [...] as well as economically these people are set to defy the authority of the Union and Mandate Government." When Naude challenged the brewers with these accusations, "Sickel nearly went on his knees to try and persuade me to keep the case out of court. He assured me that the Brewery would pay anything to keep the case out of Court." Naude advises however to follow the law as rigidly as possible. NAN, SWAA 3115, Monthly Revenue Returns: Alleged customs fraud Hansa Brewery Swakopmund: Sgd. J.W. Naude, Inspector. District Commandant, Omaruru, 24/02/1939, to the Commissioner, South West Africa Police.

[42] NAN, SWAA 2572, Trading with the enemy. Hansa Breweries, Swakopmund: The Secretary for South West Africa in Windhoek, 30/09/1940, to the Secretary for Commerce and Industries in Pretoria.

[43] NAN, SWAA 2572, Trading with the enemy. Hansa Breweries, Swakopmund: J.L. Human, Secretary for South West Africa, 30/09/1940, to the Administrator in Windhoek; Secretary for Commerce and Industries, 23/07/1940, to the Secretary, office of the High Commissioner, South Africa House, London.

[44] NAN, SWAA 2572, Trading with the enemy. Hansa Breweries, Swakopmund: Secretary for Commerce and Industries, 27/04/1940, to the Secretary, office of the High Commissioner, South Africa House, London.

[45] Including two shareholders of Hansa Brewery. Two other shareholders were marked down for internment, but because of their young age had been put on strict parole instead. NAN, SWAA 2572, Trading with the enemy. Hansa Breweries, Swakopmund: The Secretary for South West Africa in Windhoek, 30/09/1940, to the Secretary for Commerce and Industries in Pretoria.

[46] H. Herre, 'Erinnerungen an die Lagerzeit in Andalusia', in: R. Kock (ed.), *Erinnerungen an die Interni-*

camps show two things. Firstly, the South Africans feared the German community and an uprising in their colony, and hence made it very difficult for brewers and Germans in general to get on with their business and their lives. Secondly, despite all the difficult challenges they were facing, people were always able to make beer if they desired to do so. The breweries evidently kept on brewing during the war years while interned Germans went underground to make liquor.

Problematic Liquor Law

After the war was over, things went back to normal. But quickly, the breweries faced another strain on their business activities: the liquor laws that South Africa imposed on the territory proved to be highly problematic. The state was very much occupied with the liquor laws and its effects on the population. Statistics from the 1950s from Windhoek show the absurd involvement of the state with alcohol. Liquor cases accounted for 57.6% of all criminal cases, while illegal drinking caused 89.4% of all fines imposed on the black population.[47]

Consuming beer illegally was by far the most criminal activity an African could do and these laws exceeded notorious apartheid rules such as the Masters and Servants Proclamation. The reason for the preoccupation of the state with alcohol was the fear of the South African government to lose control over the population. There was a deep belief that black people had a lack of discipline and self-control and were not able to drink responsibly. As a consequence, settlers feared shortages of native labour as a result of absenteeism.[48]

The tax revenues from alcohol consumption were an advantage for the state, but for the most part the liquor situation caused problems for the authorities. The law was problematic on two different levels, following the racial divide of the two beer markets. The white settlers had difficulties interpreting and applying the complicated set of laws, and moreover there were conflicting ideas within the different settler communities about the whole concept of alcohol consumption. The local population on the other hand was not allowed to drink at all, but obviously found many ways to circumvent the dreaded laws.

---

  erungszeit (1939–1946) und zeitgeschichtliche Ergänzungen (Windhoek 2003) 67–69.
[47] R. Gordon, Inside the Windhoek Lager: Liquor and Lust in Namibia, in: W. Jankowiak and D. Bradburd (eds.) *Drugs, labor, and colonial expansion* (Tucson 2003) 117–126.
[48] Gordon describes the so-called "crisis in drinking" and colonial fears in more detail. R. Gordon, Inside the Windhoek Lager, 117–126.

The White Population

First of all, there was much discontent within the white settler communities. The administration had difficulties interpreting the set of laws, since the liquor laws formed a highly complex judicial system. The Proclamation of 1920, which we saw at the start of this chapter, proposed quite a simple distinction between Europeans and natives. It was already one of the longest pieces of all legislation, but despite the detailed outline, the execution of the law proved to be difficult. Consolidation of the numerous amendments took place in 1936 and 1952. In 1953, L.C. Barrett published a lengthy book with the complete law, adding all amendments, notes, relevant cases and further legislation. It is an interesting example of how lawyers and judges struggled with the interpretation.[49] G.G.R. Brebner, judge of the High Court of SWA, summarised the problem in his foreword of the book:

> Since 1920 the Liquor Licensing Proclamation has been extensively amended and it became a tedious and difficult matter to follow accurately the various amendments and additions. More than one commission was appointed to recommend changes of the law.[50]

The government was not only struggling with the judicial interpretation of the law, there were also problems with the whole concept of the liquor legislation in itself, as it caused discontent within the white settler communities. Also in 1953, the Administrator of SWA appointed a Commission of Enquiry to discuss the sale of liquor, one of the key issues of the administration.[51] The police, municipalities, church denominations, sporting bodies and hotels were represented in the Commission, and the various actors discussed important matters such as the problems of intoxicating liquor, the rules for bottle stores and the exclusion of women from bars.[52] The final report shows that the administration faced severe difficulties with the current liquor situation. More specifically, it signalled a gap between South African culture and German and English settler segments of SWA.

The Commission of Enquiry noticed that: "In this Territory there is generally speaking a clash between the original German culture and the new Afrikaans culture."[53] The

---

[49] NAN, F002-AA/1996, The liquor law of South-West Africa: being the Liquor Licensing Proclamation, 1920 (Proclamation no.6 of 1920), as amended from time to time, with notes, references to decided casses [sic] and other relevant legislation.
[50] NAN, F002-AA/1996, The liquor law of South-West Africa: being the Liquor Licensing Proclamation, 1920 (Proclamation no.6 of 1920) V.
[51] Gordon provides a short historical background on the emergence of the Commission: R. Gordon, Inside the Windhoek Lager: Liquor and Lust in Namibia, in: W. Jankowiak and D. Bradburd (eds.) *Drugs, labor, and colonial expansion* (Tucson 2003) 128–132.
[52] During these years, the law only allowed men into bars. As a result, women and children had to sit on the veranda or in the hotel lounge. I thank Gunter von Schumann for pointing this out to me.
[53] NAN, F002-L.0781a, Commission of Enquiry: Sale of liquor and desecration of Sunday.

administration aimed to use beer as a political instrument with South African inspired liquor legislation. These aspirations clashed not only with the local population, but also with non-Afrikaans white settlers, who, according to the report, had developed a distinctive culture over the years.[54] The Commission noted that "It is very difficult for somebody from the Union to adapt himself to local conditions," implicating that the legislators might be ill-informed.[55] To quote from the report of the Commission:

> South West Africa has its own traditions which are modelled on those of Germany. Contact with the Union and with Afrikaans traditions is more recent, and consequently there is a conflict of ideas in more than one respect.[56]

The Black Population

Secondly, it became clear that the legislation did not affect the local population as it was intended to. The legislative loophole of home brewing became highly troublesome, because many locals were able to circumvent the law. Home brewing grew tremendously and in the eyes of white settlers, indigenes were excessive and irresponsible drinkers.[57] The smuggling of beer occurred regularly in the northern part of SWA, where cuca beer from Angola was transported over the border.[58] This is the reason why today shebeens in the north of Namibia are generally called cuca shops.

The government opted for a 'carrot and stick method' in order to push the black population back in line. The liquor law crumbled before the eyes of the administration and their response was twofold. On the one hand, the state reacted with force, while on the other hand an alternative was offered. The 'stick' consisted of a harsh government reaction to home brewing, for instance with notorious liquor raids.[59] In 1947, the government

---

[54] R. Gordon, Inside the Windhoek Lager: Liquor and Lust in Namibia, in: W. Jankowiak and D. Bradburd (eds.) *Drugs, labor, and colonial expansion* (Tucson 2003) 130.
[55] NAN, F002-L.0781a, Commission of Enquiry: Sale of liquor and desecration of Sunday.
[56] Ibid.
[57] R. Gordon, Inside the Windhoek Lager: Liquor and Lust in Namibia, in: W. Jankowiak and D. Bradburd (eds.) *Drugs, labor, and colonial expansion* (Tucson 2003) 126.
[58] H. Siiskonen, 'Namibia and the Heritage of Colonial Alcohol Policy', *Nordic Journal of African Studies* Vol. 3 No. 1 (1994) 78. It was also noted by the government that cases of liquor were smuggled over the border, see: NAN, SWAA 150, Ovamboland. Distilling of alcohol by natives: Extract from quarterly report by the native commissioner, Ondangua, Ovamboland, for the quarter ended 31st March, 1949.
[59] J.B. Gewald, 'Diluting Drinks and Deepening Discontent: Colonial Liquor Controls and Public Resistance in Windhoek, Namibia', in: D. Bryceson (eds.), *Alcohol in Africa: Mixing Business, Pleasure, and Politics* (Portsmouth 2002) 126; R. Gordon, Inside the Windhoek Lager: Liquor and Lust in Namibia, in: W. Jankowiak and D. Bradburd (eds.) *Drugs, labor, and colonial expansion* (Tucson 2003) 127–128; 'NAN, JUS 156, Kaffir beer: From C.F. Marais and P.J. Koen, 07/11/1957 or 13/11/1957, to the Administrator-In-Executive Committee.

demolished 352 brewing facilities in Ovamboland — in six months' time.[60] The Native Commissioner invited the headmen of Ovamboland to read Article 3 of the Mandate Agreement, to remind them of the law.[61]

The state started to take an active interest in home brewing and sent samples of drinks to laboratories in South Africa for an analysis of the alcohol content.[62] the state's occupation with home brewing is also shown by the aforementioned crime statistics from the 1950s, which showed that liquor cases accounted for roughly 60% of all criminal cases and that roughly 90% of all fines imposed on the black population were caused by illegal drinking.[63]

The best example of the 'stick' is perhaps a piece of legislation called the "Dried Peas Control Ordinance" from 1957. Dried peas constituted one of the main ingredients for making a home brewed version of beer. This piece of legislation declared that dried peas could not be sold, delivered, given or otherwise supplied to any "native."[64] The opposition against this law came, surprisingly, from the (white) Chambers of Commerce. The Chamber of Commerce in Walvisbay wrote a lengthy response to the government concerning the Ordinance, starting with the point that for the "coloured"[65] fishermen in Walvis Bay, dried peas were a necessary foodstuff. It was requested that the Ordinance would only count for the Ovambo, since they were expected to be the main brewers. But most importantly, the Chamber argued that the Ordinance was putting the stores in an "extremely difficult position" because the shopkeepers had to decide who fell under the category of native.[66]

> Many Europeans who look like near whites make it difficult [...] to decide correctly into which class they fall. Grocery assistants and even Grocery Managers would constantly be involved in embarrassing situations.[67]

---

[60] NAN, NAO 071, Native Customs and Practices, Distilling Alcohol: Note from 29/8/47; H.L.P. Eedes, Native Commissioner in Ondangua, 12/09/1947, to the Chief Native Commissioner in Windhoek; NAN, SWAA 1504, Ovamboland. Distilling of alcohol by natives: Extract from quarterly report. Quarter April – September, 1947. Native commissioner, Ondangua, Ovamboland.

[61] NAN, NAO 071, Native Customs and Practices, Distilling Alcohol: The Native Commissioner in Ondangua, 12/05/1947, to the Assistant Native Commissioner in Oshikango.

[62] NAN, NAO 071, Native Customs and Practices, Distilling Alcohol: H.L.P. Eedes, Native Commissioner Ovamboland in Ondangua, 05/02/1949, to the Chief Native Commissioner in Windhoek, and several other small notes and letters in this archival file.

[63] R. Gordon, Inside the Windhoek Lager: Liquor and Lust in Namibia, in: W. Jankowiak and D. Bradburd (eds.) *Drugs, labor, and colonial expansion* (Tucson 2003) 117–126.

[64] NAN, JUS 156, Kaffir beer: Dried Peas Control Ordinance 1957.

[65] The apartheid administration divided people into racial categories: whites, blacks, coloureds and Asians.

[66] NAN, JUS 156, Kaffir beer: From C.F. Marais and P.J. Koen, 7/11/1957 or 13/11/1957, to the Administrator-In-Executive Committee.

[67] NAN, JUS 156, Kaffir beer: From C.F. Marais and P.J. Koen, 7/11/1957 or 13/11/1957, to the Administrator-In-Executive Committee.

Chambers of Commerce from other towns rebelled against the Ordinance as well. The Chamber of Commerce in Outjo complained that shopkeepers were left with large amounts of stock that became less valuable.[68] Otjiwarongo had similar complaints.[69] The Chamber of Commerce in Swakopmund went the furthest, asking for a complete repeal of the law.[70] None of these requests were met by the government.

The government's response to the embarrassed shop owners in Walvis Bay was significant. The Magistrate of Walvis Bay referred the matter to the District Commandant of the South African Police in Omaruru. The solution was simple, according to the police. When a shop owner was not sure about the 'whiteness' of a customer, "an excuse could always be made that the commodity is out of stock so as to avoid giving offence."[71] In other words: nothing changed and any comments from the shopkeepers was not appreciated. The Chamber in Walvis Bay noted in a dreary reply that the brewing of illicit beer had not been curbed since the Ordinance came into being.[72] It is a strange fact that the Dread Peas Control Ordinance has not yet been formally repealed since Namibia became independent — in theory, the legislation is still intact today.[73]

The 'carrot,' on the other hand, consisted of beer halls. A beer hall was a place where black Africans could drink beer under the supervision of the state. It was some sort of perceived stepping stone towards the drinking of European beers. The beer halls sold an imitation of "kaffir beer," which was in judicial terms the beer "commonly brewed by natives from kaffir corn or millet or other grain and not containing more than 3% by weight of alcohol."[74] Sometimes "kaffir" is used as a universal name for drinks such as *ertjies beer, karrie, !Khari, Otjikariha, bantubeer* and other variants. It was a popular concoction made from several ingredients, ranging from potatoes, peas, and beans to mealies and more, and

---

[68] NAN, JUS 156, Kaffir beer: Die Sekretaris, Ordonnansie om die verkoop van droë ertjies te beheer.
[69] NAN, JUS 156, Kaffir beer: Secretary of South West Africa, P.J. Koen in Windhoek, 14/09/1957, to the Secretary of the Chamber of Commerce in Otjiwarongo.
[70] NAN, JUS 156, Kaffir beer: Chamber of Commerce in Swakopmund, 04/06/1957, to the Secretary for South West Africa.
[71] NAN, JUS 156, Kaffir beer: From C.F. Marais and P.J. Koen, 7/11/1957 or 13/11/1957, to the Administrator-In-Executive Committee.
[72] Ibid.
[73] The Namibian reported in 2014 that the Law Reform and Development Commission identified that the Dried Peas Control Ordinance was never formally repealed. Ellison Tjirera wrote in an Insight Namibia issue from December 2015 – January 2015 that this is still the case. The Liquor Act No. 6 of 1998 repealed the Kaffir Beer Control Ordinance and thereby legally reformed the liquor industry. For unknown reasons the Dried Peas Control Ordinance remained and is still to be found in Namibia's statute books. W. Menges, 'Native? Sorry, no dried peas', *The Namibian*, 22nd August 2014; E. Tjirera, 'Dried peas and the politics of inebriation', *Insight Namibia*, December 2015 – January 2016.
[74] NAN, JUS 156, Kaffir beer: Ordinance to provide for the brewing of Kaffir beer by natives on land outside urban area; and other legislative texts.

Fig. 23: Beer is being served in the municipal beer hall in Windhoek, 1953.

for the fermentation sugar, golden syrup or other fermenting substances were used.[75] It was a relatively cheap drink.[76]

Beer halls could be found all over SWA.[77] In every major "location" (township) of a town, a beer hall was placed. The model came from South Africa, where beer halls were a common feature of the daily lives of black Africans.[78] The municipality of Windhoek approached the brewers of SWB to make an imitation of the local "kaffir beer" for the planned beer hall in Windhoek's Location.[79] In 1934, a batch of 1000 litres was produced

---

[75] NAN F002-RARA/062, Native beverages 1931: 3.
[76] NAN, MTS 8, Non-European Affairs: Beer Hall: Lokasiesuperintendent, 11/05/1970, to the Stadsklerk in Tsumeb.
[77] The National Archives contain numerous files on beer halls and this constitutes a tremendous separate research topic.
[78] P. la Hausse, 'Drink and Cultural Innovation in Durban: The Origins of the Beerhall in South Africa, 1902–1916', in: J. Crush and C. Ambler (eds.), *Liquor and Labor in Southern Africa* (Athens 1992); WCARS, CMT 3/1086, Liquor: kaffir beer. General; WCARS, 3/CT, 4/1/9/1/137, Liquor. Proposed establishment of bantu beer brewery (also tour of up country establishments re same) [sic].
[79] The location was the township where all black people were forced to live. Every town in SWA had a location.

Fig. 24: Customers are drinking beer from tins in the beer hall in the Old Location, Windhoek.

and supplied to the Location Advisory Board for tasting. This institution was introduced by the South African authorities as a means to extend their control over the black African population. Board members were appointed by the colonial administration or would be voted in by elections that were only open to men.[80] The Advisory Board held meetings to discuss the quality of the brew. A municipal policeman, who was not on the board, presented his views on the taste of the liquor: "The beer is very clean and pure, just as clean and pure as the water in the tanks and has the same strength. […] I know what liquor is and the beer supplied is no stronger than water."[81]

The test brew was clearly of an unsatisfactorily quality and it took a while before a final brew was chosen. It was not easy for the official brewers to fulfil this specific task. Two years later, the Secretary for SWA wrote to government officials in Pretoria that a loss in beer could

---

[80] J.B. Gewald, 'Diluting Drinks and Deepening Discontent: Colonial Liquor Controls and Public Resistance in Windhoek, Namibia', in: D. Bryceson (ed.), *Alcohol in Africa: Mixing Business, Pleasure, and Politics* (Portsmouth 2002) 119.
[81] Ibid. 130, quote by Corporal Petrus.

Fig. 25: One of the many shebeens in Namibia.

be partly explained by the "inexperience in brewing Kaffir beer" of the SWB brewers.[82] In 1936, the municipal beer hall of Windhoek was opened, which G.O. Bowker, the superintendent of the township, saw as an exercise in "civilizing the native." The beer hall was always a contested place, one where beer and politics intermingled.[83]

Over the course of time, all major townships in SWA had a beer hall. In effect, the revenues derived from the drinking of beer were used to fund apartheid amenities. Mager, a historian who wrote extensively on the South African beer market and the history of South African Breweries in particular, came to a similar conclusion when she examined the beer halls in South Africa. Her conclusion was as grim as it was true: "Africans were drinking themselves into the Apartheid system."[84]

A solution was found for the people outside the towns, who did not have access to the beer halls. With the Kaffir Beer (Rural Areas) Control Ordinance of 1957 it became pos-

---

[82] NAN, SWAA 3113, Customs and Excise: Brewery regulations: The Secretary for South West Africa in Windhoek, 07/08/1936, to the Commissioner of Customs & Excise in Pretoria.

[83] J.B. Gewald, 'Diluting Drinks and Deepening Discontent: Colonial Liquor Controls and Public Resistance in Windhoek, Namibia', in: D. Bryceson (ed.), *Alcohol in Africa: Mixing Business, Pleasure, and Politics* (Portsmouth 2002) 131.

[84] A. Mager, 'The First Decade of 'European Beer' in Apartheid South Africa: The State, the Brewers and the Drinking Public, 1962–72', *The Journal of African History* Vol. 40 No. 3 (1999) 382–383.

sible for locals to brew beer on land outside an urban area, as long as they had a written consent from the European landowner.[85] People were slowly warming towards the idea that beer could become legal. In response to a proposed amendment of the liquor act in 1956, the Office of the Magistrate in Omaruru wrote to the Secretary of SWA: "In any case you will never stop them brewing potent liquor. In my opinion they should be allowed to purchase the ordinary liquor." It took however more than a decade before this idea became a reality.[86]

The Change of the 1960s

The 1960s changed everything for SWA. The armed struggle for independence commenced in 1966, when the South West Africa People's Organisation (SWAPO) engaged in military contact with South African forces for the first time. SWAPO was the main liberation movement of SWA and was born out of several smaller organisations that were mainly based in the northern part of SWA, called Ovamboland. Over the years, SWAPO became internationally recognised as the representative of the people of SWA. The year 1966 was the start of a long guerrilla war against the South African apartheid government, whereby most of the SWAPO forces were forced into exile.

In 1967, the List family acquired the majority shareholding of SWB. When Carl List, co-founder of the company together with Hermann Ohlthaver, died in 1959, his son Karl Werner List took over. The company's history so far was a history of family fights: several wealthy families tried to obtain power over the brewing concern. Werner List also had to share his power with other families, but thanks to his wife Hilde, this was about to change.

At this point in time, a man called E.A.H.F. Behnsen was the chairman of the board.[87] List's wife, Hilde, travelled all over the country to talk to shareholders of SWB and she was able to persuade them to sell the shares to her husband. She did not have much money, but the O&L group could finance the trade with their own shares. As a result, List was able to acquire a majority in shares. According to the stories, List was now able to walk into the boardroom and tell Behnsen that he was his new boss — which he did. Less known is however the crucial role that Hilde played in Werner's attempt to gain control.[88]

---

[85] NAN, JUS 156, Kaffir beer: Kaffir Beer (Rural Areas) Control Ordinance, 1957.
[86] NAN, JUS 156, Kaffir beer: Office of the Magistrate in Omaruru, 15/10/1956, to the Secretary for South West Africa (Justice Section) in Windhoek.
[87] The Behnsen family owned Metje + Ziegler, a major company that still exists in Namibia.
[88] Interview with Bernd Masche, 22nd January 2016.

Also in 1967, SWB bought out its rival Hansa Brewery, again with the help of Hilde List.[89] With the newly acquired power within SWB, Werner List was able to merge SWB with its only remaining competitor in the territory. Other parties were also interested in Hansa Brewery prior to the merger of 1967, there were for example talks between Hansa and a company in Stellenbosch, but in the end SWB managed to incorporate Hansa Brewery. The amalgamation of the two companies was organised through an exchange of shares between Hansa shares and SWB shares. The main reason behind this procedure was, according to the manager of Hansa Brewery, Ernst Heuschneider, the threat of SAB (the following chapter will deal with this more extensively). The relatively small turnover of Hansa is also named as a reason. The two companies were formally one, but were still able to function independently from each other.[90]

Finally, in the year 1969, the South African government officially repealed the racial Liquor Licensing Proclamation. This means that the alcohol prohibition came to an end, allowing black consumers to legally buy the European style commercial beer that was being brewed by SWB and Hansa Brewery.[91] This in turn led to the establishment of thousands of illicit bars where the local communities could buy and drink beer.[92] These bars, currently known as shebeens or cuca shops, can still be found all over the country.

In conclusion, the beer market changed completely in the fifty years' time between 1920 and 1970. At the start of this era, the market consisted of three breweries that were competitors (SWB, Union Brewery and Hansa Brewery). But in 1970, only one brewing company remained. Furthermore, this era started out with two racially divided beer markets: one formal market for the white settler community, and one informal market for the black population. In 1970, only one market remained because the black population was finally allowed to legally drink beer. When the year of 1970 commenced, SWA had a single brewing group that could cater for the whole population.

---

[89] NAN, F002-PC/0044, South West Breweries gazette.
[90] Interview Brenda Bravenboer with Ernst Heuschneider, 27th February 2012.
[91] Again, South Africa was the example, where the prohibition ended in 1962. See A. Mager, 'The First Decade of 'European Beer' in Apartheid South Africa: The State, the Brewers and the Drinking Public, 1962–72', *The Journal of African History* Vol. 40 No. 3 (1999) 367–388.
[92] H. Siiskonen, 'Namibia and the Heritage of Colonial Alcohol Policy', *Nordic Journal of African Studies* Vol. 3 No. 1 (1994) 80.

3 Namibia Breweries' Transformation, 1970–2019

SWB already existed for fifty years when the brewing company entered this time period. In many ways, the company was facing a new situation. After decades of domestic competition, it remained as the only commercial brewing company left in the country, since Hansa Brewery had been bought out and was now part of the company. Lastly, and perhaps most importantly, the black population was legally allowed to acquire and consume the beers that were produced in Windhoek and Swakopmund. In other words, the possible consumer base of SWB had increased dramatically.

It seemed like SWB had a bright future ahead, but appearances can be deceptive. Around this time, a rivalling company stepped into the limelight, namely South African Breweries (SAB). This enormous brewing company, based in South Africa, formed a major threat to the local brewing practices in SWA. This last chapter of the book explains how the brewers of SWB were able to transform their company and use a series of historical events for their own advantage, thereby saving the existence of the company.

A South West Company

Around the 1970s, SWB was still very much seen as a 'South West company,' meaning that its identity was closely linked to the white settlers of SWA. The brewery produced beer for a relatively small group of consumers, namely the white population of mainly German and South African (Afrikaans) descent. The company's name was modelled after the current racial political administration and the beer was promoted as the "true South West Beer," a name that became a settler catchword around the territory.[1]

An article in the South West Africa Annual, a tri-lingual periodical that "played an important role in promoting and strengthening a sense of 'South West' identity in Namibia's settler society," highlights SWB's image.[2] The beer was hailed as the "national drink" of the South Westers in an article with the roaring title "The Proud Boast and Toast of South West Africa Is Its Glorious Beer." The text furthermore stated:

---

[1] R. Gordon., Inside the Windhoek Lager: Liquor and Lust in Namibia, in: W. Jankowiak and D. Bradburd (eds.) *Drugs, labor, and colonial expansion* (Tucson 2003) 132.

[2] Suidwes-Afrika-Jaarboek, 1953. Besides articles, every edition of the South West Africa Annual featured advertisements from South West Breweries. According to Carl Schlettwein, this was a must for some companies, "not with the aim of increasing sales, but to underline their identity as part of colonial Namibia." G. Miescher, L Rizzo and J. Silvester, 'Carl Schlettwein — Commercial Advertising in Namibia in the 1950s', in: G. Miescher, L Rizzo and J. Silvester (eds.), *Posters in Action* (Basel 2009) 110–111.

> For more than 50 years beer has been the national beverage of South West Africa. In fact, it might well be described as a national food. [...] There is much that is sound in the contention that beer produced in South West Africa is a national beverage.[3]

SWB beer became an icon of the national identity of these white South Westers.[4] Many settler traditions that came to define their community were entangled with the presence of SWB beer:

> Once a year a 'Bockbier' is produced. This is a dark beer, very heavy, and its appearance for sale results in many a 'Bock Bier Fest.' Usually this is combined with a 'Schlachtefest.' Enterprising hoteliers and many private people slaughter pigs and prepare various pork dishes and, of course, pork sausages. These are served with masses of sauerkraut, washed down with copious draughts of 'Mai Bock.' [...] Beer is also an important adjunct to a 'Richtefest' (roof wetting). No building is considered properly established without a roof wetting and this consists of large quantities of beer served with Vienna sausages, fresh, crisp rolls and adequate helpings of mustard.[5]

In other words, beer became indispensable for various traditions that were important for South Western culture. When one travelled by train from South Africa back to the familiar South West Africa, a glass of local beer was the symbol of coming home:

> An interesting vignette of the attitude of residents of the Territory towards their own beer is noticeable on trains leaving De Aar [Northern Cape, South Africa] for Windhoek. No sooner does the returning South West African board the train he immediately demands 'a cold South West beer.'[6]

There is not a better embodiment for this observation than the brewery's logo, which contained the image of the Equestrian Monument (better known as the Reiterdenkmal or Südwester Reiter). It is a statue that commemorates the Germans whom died during the genocide of the Herero and the Nama between 1904 and 1908.[7] The monument was inaugurated in 1912, on the birthday of the German emperor Wilhelm II, and displays a soldier on horseback. Governor Theodor Seitz stated in his inauguration speech in 1912: "The bronze horseman of the colonial forces surveys the land from this place and proclaims to the world that we are and shall remain masters here."[8]

---

[3] NSS, South West Africa Annual, 1953.
[4] R. Gordon, Inside the Windhoek Lager: Liquor and Lust in Namibia, in: W. Jankowiak and D. Bradburd (eds.) *Drugs, labor, and colonial expansion* (Tucson 2003) 132.
[5] NSS, South West Africa Annual, 1953.
[6] Ibid.
[7] G. von Schumann and G. McGregor, *The Equestrian Monument (Reiterdenkmal) 1912–2014: A chronological documentation of reports, newspaper clippings and photos/illustrations* (Windhoek 2014).
[8] J. Zeller, 'Symbol politics: Notes on the German colonial culture of remembrance', in: J. Zimmerer and WWWJ. Zeller, *Genocide in German South-West Africa: The Colonial War of 1904–1908 And Its Aftermath* (Berlin 2003) 231.

Fig. 26: A bottle of Windhoek Lager, displaying the Reiter on the logo of South West Breweries.

Figure 27: The beer coasters of South West Breweries promoted SWB beer as 'The Genuine South West Beer'. Again, the Reiter is featured as well.

The monument has been controversial for a long time, as it is seen as a symbol of colonial victory, oppression and foreign rule.[9] Especially after independence, the statue became a topic of debate and strongly divided the Namibian population.[10] In 2013, the statue was unexpectedly removed by the SWAPO government and was stored in the

---

[9] As argued by Zeller and others: J. Zeller, 'Symbol politics: Notes on the German colonial culture of remembrance' 231–251.

[10] The population from German descent was also divided over the question what should happen with this statue. E. Zuern, 'Memorial politics: challenging the dominant party's narrative in Namibia', *The Journal of Modern African Studies* Vol. 40 No. 03 (2012) 493–518. Some parts of society thought of the Reiter as a "monument for all," G. von Schumann and G. McGregor, *The Equestrian Monument (Reiterdenkmal) 1912–2014: A chronological documentation of reports, newspaper clippings and photos/illustrations* (Windhoek 2014). The former Managing Director of SWB, Bernd Masche, strongly believes that the statue is a monument for all parts of society and should not be associated with the genocide. Interview with Bernd Masche, 22nd January 2016.

Alte Feste on Christmas Eve. The police cordoned off the area in order to prevent the public from getting close to the monument.[11] For decades, including during the 1970s when SWB became the national brewer, "the Reiter" was not only the symbol of colonial administration and racial laws, but also the symbol of the brewery. Every bottle, coaster and poster featured this monument prominently.

Challenge from South African Breweries

In the meantime, a new challenge to the near monopoly of SWB emerged in the form of SAB. The big rival from the neighbouring South Africa eagerly wanted to enter the South Western market. SAB was nothing more but a brewing giant, a company that at this point in time owned more than 90% of the whole southern African beer market.[12] The battle that broke out between the two rivals came to define SWB and in part the Namibian beer market as well.

It is a curious fact that, historically, SAB used to own shares from SWB, although the exact details of this cooperation remain mysterious. The management group that was in charge of the brewery during the 1970s and 1980s vividly remember that SAB had a 25% shareholding of SWB, but has trouble recalling the exact details.[13] According to the website of SAB, a minority shareholding of SWB was acquired in 1965.[14] While the reason for this development remains unclear, it is plausible that SWB sought to attract capital and therefore offered the sale of shares to outside investors. The major project that both companies undertook was the launch of a new beer brand for the Southern African market, called Hansa Pilsener. This beer was brewed at the Hansa Brewery in Swakopmund and was sold in South West Africa, whilst SAB had a royalty

---

[11] The Alte Feste was a German fort and the very first stone building of Windhoek. The Schutztruppe, German troops, were stationed here. The Alte Feste was situated on a hill in Windhoek and overlooked the larger area. It still exists, although there is not much to see. The National Museum was situated in the Alte Feste until it was moved. Currently the building is gradually falling apart.

[12] Interviews with Bernd Masche, 22nd January and 15th February 2016.

[13] It is problematic that the company archive of NBL is not intact anymore. After the moving of the brewery from Tal Street to Iscor Street, many documents were lost. Former and current employees of SAB and NBL confirm, however, that there was an agreement between SAB and SWB. Interview with Bernd Masche, 22nd January 2016; Interview with Bogart Butler and Linda Buckingham, 17th February 2016; Interview Brenda Bravenboer with Ernst Heuschneider, 27th February 2012; Interview Brenda Bravenboer with Helmut Pfaller, 26th May 2015; Interview Brenda Bravenboer with Ernst Ender, 22nd May 2015; Interview with Bogart Butler and Linda Buckingham, 17th February 2016.

[14] An extensive online SAB timeline, ranging from 1886 to 2012, mentions a "Minority investment taken up in South West Breweries" in the year 1965. The timeline is difficult to find, one copy is available on the website of SABMiller Romania, accessed 5th July 2016: http://ursus-breweries.ro/sabmiller-in-lume/istoric/?lng=2.

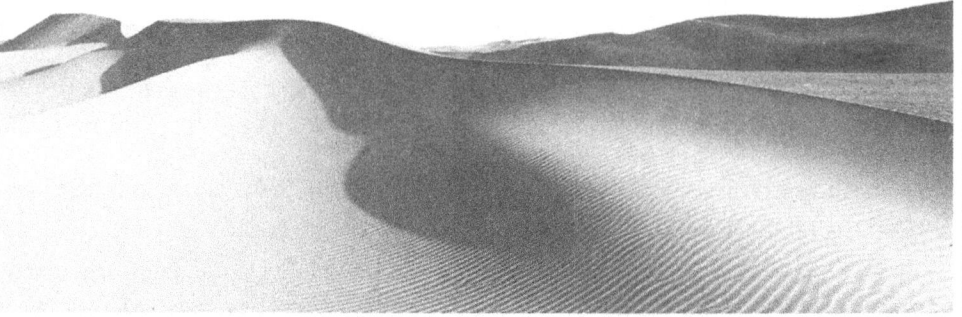

Fig. 28: A poster of Hansa Pilsener.

agreement with Hansa Brewery to brew and sell the Hansa Pilsener exclusively in South Africa. According to the brand's website, the product was first introduced in South Africa in 1975.[15]

The cooperation between SAB and SWB did not constitute a healthy relationship and the cooperation slowly dissolved over time. According to Bernd Masche, the managing director of SWB during this time, the relationship became more and more sour.[16] List, the chairman of the SWB board, did not pay dividend to the shareholders of SWB, causing irritation at SAB. The South African brewing company was an important shareholder and wanted more power. In turn, the SAB management was being accused of blocking important decisions for SWB, for instance concerning certain alterations in the Articles of Association that were necessary to increase the borrowing powers of SWB.[17] In short, the brewers at SWB felt that SAB simply wanted a quick return on their investment, something they could not offer as a result of the challenging economic conditions.[18]

The breaking point of this smouldering conflict was reached during the construction of the new SWB brewing complex, halfway through the 1980s. A new brewery was being built by SWB in Windhoek. A hefty amount of capital was necessary for this endeavour and therefore it became crucial that the company increased its borrowing power. Changing the Articles of Association during a general meeting of the shareholders was required to allow this, but SAB opposed this decision. SWB felt that SAB simply abused its power to disrupt the operations in South West Africa.[19] A deadlock had been reached.

The solution for the troublesome situation proved to be the Hansa Pilsener brand that SAB was selling under license in South Africa. After ten years the license had to be renewed, according to the agreement made between the two companies. Instead of renewing the licence, SAB and SWB devised a clever deal. SAB received the Hansa trademark for South Africa and some of the surrounding countries, so that they could continue to brew and sell Hansa Pilsener to their customers. As part of the contract, Hansa Pilsener could not be sold in SWA by SAB. In return, SAB gave almost all of its shares back to SWB (which opened up the possibility of building a new brewery complex).[20]

---

[15] Two years after the introduction, the brand had to be relaunched, because the consumers were not buying the product. In 2001, it became the second largest beer brand in South Africa and in 2011 it was voted the most popular beer in South Africa by the Sunday Times. Hansa Pilsener website, accessed 21st May 2016: http://hansapilsener.co.za/the-beer/history.
[16] Interview with Bernd Masche, 22nd January 2016; SAB officials also confirm this: Interview with Bogart Butler and Linda Buckingham, 17th February 2016.
[17] Interview with Bernd Masche, 15th February 2016.
[18] Interview with Bernd Masche, 22nd January 2016.
[19] Interview Brenda Bravenboer with Ernst Heuschneider, 27th February 2012.
[20] SWB feared that Tafel Lager, the brand that was taken over from the Hansa Brewery, could no longer be exported to South Africa as well. After all, SAB got the "Hansa" trademark together with the Hansa

SWB was only a tiny company, as seen from a brewer's perspective. Brewing beer for just a few of the white South Westers from German descent, in practice a small consumer base scattered across a vast area, was not a viable business strategy in the long-term, especially in an industry where the economies of scale were becoming increasingly important. All over the globe, breweries were getting bigger and bigger. The involvement of SAB in SWB and its desire to acquire market share in SWA made the regional beer industry increasingly complex. The rivalry has been described as a "David versus Goliath" battle, while the "million-dollar question" for the SWB brewers was: how will their company be able to survive?

The North Opens Up

Seemingly all of a sudden, something unexpected happened: "the north opened up," as former brewers explained to me during interviews. At this point in time, half of the country's population lived in Ovamboland, in the northern part of SWA, which made this place a considerable market. Throughout history, the breweries in the central and southern parts of SWA were never able to bring their beers to this substantial group of consumers. SWB, up until the 1970s, could only cover the area that constituted the beer triangle (Swakopmund, Windhoek and Omaruru), and the surrounding rail connected towns in the territory.[21] SWB may have dominated the beer market in the sense that they were the only commercial brewery in South West Africa, but they could not cover the beer market in its entirety.

The fact that the centrally located breweries could not reach the northern market had two different reasons. First of all, the long tradition of duty-free smuggling of cuca beer across the Angolan border was a problem.[22] This is also the reason why shebeens in the north are often called cuca shops; they are named after the cuca beer. It was basically impossible to compete with this cheap beer that has historically been in Ovamboland for a long time. Cuca beer provided for 80–90% of the market in the northern part of SWA. Secondly, the brewery was unable to acquire transport licenses to transport the beer via

---

Pilsener brand. Windhoek Lager (originally from SWB) and Tafel Lager (originally from Hansa) were two of the largest brands. After the SAB agreement, SWB simply removed the name "Hansa" from the label of Tafel Lager and kept exporting this beer to the South African market. Interview with Hans Herrmann and Christian Müller, 18th November 2015; Interview with Bernd Masche, 15th February 2016; Interview with Bernd Masche, 22nd January 2016; Interview Brenda Bravenboer with Helmut Pfaller, 26th May 2015.

[21] Interview with Bernd Masche, 22nd January 2016; Interview with Bernd Masche, 15th February 2016.
[22] H. Siiskonen, 'Namibia and the Heritage of Colonial Alcohol Policy', *Nordic Journal of African Studies* Vol. 3 No. 1 (1994) 78. Interview Brenda Bravenboer with Ernst Ender, 22nd May 2015.

trucks to Ovamboland for a long time. The railways dominated the transport industry and the brewery had to deal with them, which was too expensive.[23] Thus, Windhoek Lager and Tafel Lager (the two most famous brands of South West Breweries) were not available in Ovamboland for decades.

The Angolan Civil War that broke out in 1975 changed the whole dynamics of the southern African region, including the northern part of SWA.[24] The war more or less stopped the massive smuggling of cuca beer across the border, making the market better suited for another (domestic) competitor. As a response, SWB bought two Mercedes-Benz trucks from Angolan refugees — the very first start of their own transport fleet, which later grew to a considerable size.[25] After years of negotiations, SWB received a transport license for trucks and could thus avoid the expensive railway authorities that had dominated the transport industry. The license was a big deal because it meant that the brewery was finally able to bring its beers up north. Basically, a whole new market opened up for SWB as the company could tap into a fresh market of thirsty consumers that were previously largely unfamiliar with South West beer. This made the beer market finally national in terms of its scope and provided a unique opportunity for SWB to develop their struggling business.

As a result, SWB put much effort into encouraging the northerners to buy their products and thereby increased its production tremendously.[26] A flurry of new (marketing) activities commenced, with the launch of "Wambo Lager" as its most striking example. "Wambo Lager" was a new beer brand, and it was sold in a bottle with a tropical logo consisting of palm trees and an accompanying text in Oshivambo, the common language of the peoples living in the north of South West Africa. In reality, the contents of the beer was the well-known Windhoek Lager; but the Brewery simply put a different label on the bottle to connect with the newly discovered consumer base in the north.[27]

For a brief moment, SWB even tried to compete with the so-called and locally famous cuca beer. With the help of an external company, SWB brewed a beer with a label closely resembling the original cuca beer label (originally brewed by Companhia União de Cervejas de Angola). According to former key players in the Namibian brewing industry, the collaboration between the SWB and the external company was strenuous and hence the

---

[23] Interview with Bernd Masche, 22nd January 2016; Interview Brenda Bravenboer with Ernst Heuschneider, 27th February 2012.
[24] M. Wallace, *A History of Namibia: From the Beginning to 1990* (2011 Cape Town) 279; P. Chabal and N. Vidal (eds.), *Angola: the weight of history* (London 2007); Interview Brenda Bravenboer with Ernst Ender, 22nd May 2015; Interview Brenda Bravenboer with Ernst Heuschneider, 27th February 2012.
[25] Interview Brenda Bravenboer with Ernst Ender, 22nd May 2015.
[26] Interview with Bernd Masche, 15th February 2016; Interview Brenda Bravenboer with Ernst Ender, 22nd May 2015; Interview Brenda Bravenboer with Ernst Heuschneider, 27th February 2012.
[27] Interview with Bernd Masche, 22nd January 2016; Interview with Don Stevenson, 5th February 2016.

Fig. 29: A bottle of Wambo Lager.

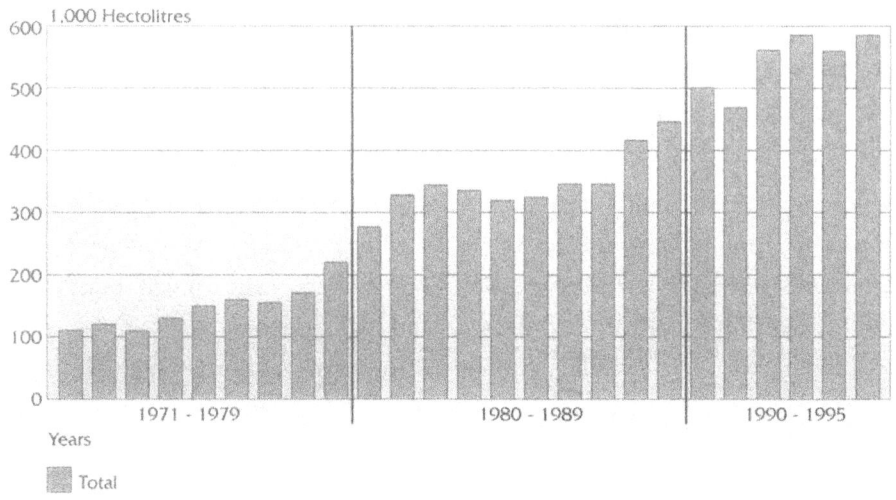

Fig. 30: The sales in beer of SWB steadily increased when the northern market opened up.

'cuca beer copy' did not work out. The external company subsequently brought the business idea to SAB, but that project failed as well.[28] Another way of connecting with the northern part of SWA was the newly erected sorghum brewery in Tsumeb, an endeavour which is discussed below.

A New Direction

The unexpected access to the consumer base in the northern part of SWA gave SWB momentum and its management decided to adopt a new direction to cope with the growing demand and simultaneously withstand the continuing threat of its rival SAB. Three factors are important in this respect. It all started with the construction of a new brewery in Windhoek, which was highly necessary because the demand for its beer was growing tremendously and production could not keep up. The new brewery subsequently allowed for a new strategy based on market differentiation via the Reinheitsgebot (purity law). Finally, the independence of Namibia in 1990 was embraced by the management and used to change the image of the company. A powerful alliance between the state and the brewery was devised in order to protect the company from outside competitors and to facilitate the export of beer to other countries, thus creating jobs and foreign exchange in return.

---

[28] Interview with Don Stevenson, former advertising director of Adfactory, 5th February 2016; Interview with Bernd Masche, 27th January 2016.

Brewery

The sudden increase in demand for SWB beers resulted in the need for a new, modern brewing plant in Windhoek. Normally, the majority of the beer production was done in the Tal Street brewery where the old Felsenkellerbrauerei was located. However, the current brewery was, in the words of the former Managing Director Masche, "a museum." The equipment was outdated and the production facilities were simply inefficient.

It was nonetheless difficult to acquire a suitable plot of land for a new brewery from Windhoek's city council, but as soon as Masche threatened to move the plant to the nearby town of Okahandja, a 10 hectare plot was organised by the council. In 1981, the company started with the construction of new and highly modern plant, located in the Northern Industrial Area of Windhoek.[29] The construction was divided into two phases. Firstly, the bottling plant was erected and was already brought into service in 1983. Secondly, the brewhouse was erected and brewing equipment was installed. In 1986, the complete brewery was finished and ready to use.[30]

Reinheitsgebot

The new brewing plant allowed the development of a new business strategy, and the key point of this strategy was to completely change the brewing process by introducing the Reinheitsgebot as the standard for the whole range of beer brands. The Reinheitsgebot was introduced to SWA after the opening of the new plant in 1986.[31] The Reinheitsgebot is a German purity law from 1516. It is often called the oldest still existing health regulation in the world.

The Reinheitsgebot prescribed that brewers could only use water, hops and malted barley. Yeast, a vital part of the brewing process, was not included. In 1516, yeast was an unknown ingredient for brewing, and was only discovered after the invention of the microscope.[32] In Germany, the Reinheitsgebot is still official law. Outside of Germany, only a few breweries choose to brew according to the strict regulations. The overarching idea of SWB was that putting an emphasis on pure beer would give the company a chance to differentiate their products from the products of SAB.

---

[29] NLN, South West Breweries Limited, Annual Report, 1981. Interview with Bernd Masche, 22nd January 2016; Interview Brenda Bravenboer with Ernst Ender, 22nd May 2015.
[30] The head engineer of the brewery, Mannfred Redecker, was responsible for the innovative roof. Interview Brenda Bravenboer with Helmut Pfaller, 26th May 2015.
[31] Interview with Hans Herrmann and Christian Müller, 18th November 2015; Interview Brenda Bravenboer with Ernst Ender, 22nd May 2015.
[32] Antony van Leeuwenhoek recorded the first microscopy study of yeast in fermenting beer in a letter to Thomas Gale, written on the 14th June 1680. J.R. Porter, 'Antony van Leeuwenhoek: Tercentenary of His Discovery of Bacteria', *Bacteriological Reviews* Vol. 40 No. 2 (1976) 265.

Fig. 31: The machinery of the old SWB brewery on Tal Street, Windhoek.

Brewing beer according to the Reinheitsgebot had three major advantages for SWB. Firstly, their products could now be moved into the premium quality segment of the market, thereby distinguishing their drinks from its competitor SAB. According to Helmut Pfaller, the master brewer of SWB during the introduction of the Reinheitsgebot, the beers of SAB and SWB were fairly similar before the introduction of the Reinheitsgebot.[33] SWB used various brewing ingredients that were not considered part of the purity law, such as sugar, maize, rice and syrup.[34] SAB had similar practices and today still uses maize or maize extract as a main ingredient for its brands such as Carling Black Label. With the Reinheitsgebot, SWB differentiated their beers in an increasingly competitive international beer market.[35]

Secondly, the focus on pure beer connected with an increasing group of consumers that favoured a healthy lifestyle. A global health movement was developing in the 1980s. Beer brewed according to the Reinheitsgebot is expected to be healthier and more nutri-

---

[33] Interview Brenda Bravenboer with Helmut Pfaller, 26th May 2015.
[34] NAN, SWAA 3113, Customs and Excise: Brewery Regulations: Breweries, 01/05/1928.
[35] Interview with Hans Herrmann and Christian Müller, 18th November 2015; Interview with Bernd Masche, 22nd January 2016; Interview Brenda Bravenboer with Ernst Ender, 22nd May 2015.

tious than other production methods because it does not involve the use of additives.[36] The brewery came up with special advertisements to promote their beer as a wholesome and nutritious drink. The great advantages, according to the advertisements "proven by medical research," were explicitly emphasised: drinking beer would lead to greater life expectancy, it was a tonic for sleeplessness and a statement was made that beer drinkers are less prone to illness.[37]

Thirdly, the Reinheitsgebot saved a massive amount of money in excise duty and made it therefore easier to export the beers abroad, more specifically to South Africa. Excise duty regimes were based on percentages of alcohol. With the new brewing recipes, the SWB beers were lower in alcohol than competitive brands (roughly 4% against 5% alcohol). This saved considerable amounts of money in terms of excise duty and gave SWB a competitive advantage.[38]

Introducing the Reinheitsgebot to SWA was a process that took a few years. SWB started changing its recipes while brewing in the old Tal Street plant and designed the new plant in a way that would facilitate the new brewing methods and techniques. After a few years of testing, the purity law could already be introduced and marketed with confidence. It was of vital importance that the purity law claim was substantiated with facts, according to former SWB brewers. SWB thus appointed Werner Schmidt, a brewing consultant from Germany, to check if the beer was really made according to the Reinheitsgebot. Only after an official certificate was issued, the brewery allowed itself to market their beers accordingly.[39] The first Reinheitsgebot marketing campaigns were rolled out in 1994.[40]

Namibian Independence
The road to Namibian independence was fraught with uncertainties for the country as a whole, including major businesses such as SWB.[41] The brewery first had a cautious

---

[36] Interview with Bernd Masche, 22nd January 2016.
[37] NAN, F002-PC/0044, South West Breweries gazette. In a quarterly review of the Namibia Foundation, Bernd Masche even says that "Drinking up to a litre of Windhoek Lager a day (…) could increase one's life expectancy, rather than do any harm!" NAN, F002-cp (in: JZ/0203) New sparkle for Namibian beer, 1985, Namibia Brief.
[38] Interview with Bernd Masche, 22nd January 2016.
[39] Interview with Bernd Masche, 22nd January 2016; Interview with Bernd Masche, 27th January 2016; Interview Brenda Bravenboer with Ernst Ender, 22nd May 2015; Interview Brenda Bravenboer with Helmut Pfaller, 26th May 2015.
[40] Interview with Bernd Masche, 22nd January 2016.
[41] Chairman Werner List writes in his annual report of 1979 that "The uncertainty regarding the political future of the Territory of South West Africa/Namibia remained unresolved." It is interesting that he already uses both South West Africa and Namibia in this official document. NLN, South West Breweries Limited, Annual Report, 1979. Three years later List writes: "[U]nfortunately I cannot foresee an early

attitude towards the impending independence as it feared an uncertain outcome, but later in time SWB viewed the political change as an opportunity to renew its identity as a company and forge new alliances. In June 1971, the International Court of Justice declared the occupation of SWA by South Africa as illegal. The General Assembly of the United Nations similarly condemned the occupation.[42] International pressure on South Africa was intensified but it took decades before independence was reached. The fight for independence was dominated by the SWAPO, a movement that has been the ruling political party of Namibia since 1990.[43]

The main question was how SWB would deal with the major political change that constituted political independence from South Africa, and finally arrived in 1990. During the 1980s, it was not easy for the SWB managers to cope with the ongoing liberation struggle. One reason was the fear that SWAPO operations would disrupt business, because the freedom fighters of SWAPO were known to plant landmines on non-tarred roads. The SWB drivers did not dare to drive their trucks filled with beer anymore, until SWB transformed the trucks into mine-proof vehicles.[44] But the main reasons were the uncertain future and an increasingly complex political arena.

One might interpret the attitude of the brewery management towards the Namibian liberation struggle as passive, because it opted for a rather passive approach towards the inevitable date of independence. This is illustrated by a contested discussion during the 1980s, when the (external) marketing company that advised SWB proposed to the board to change the brewery's Reiterdenkmal logo and prepare plans for independence. According to Don Stevenson, the advertisement director of the company that produced most of SWB's marketing materials, the brewery management did not accept this plan[45], although former SWB employees dispute this statement. The explanation for this seemingly reluctant attitude was, according to former managing director Masche, that before independence it was uncertain what direction SWAPO and the new government would take once they would gain power and that the brewery should take a non-political stance.[46]

---

peaceful solution." The beer sales increased, however, by 21% during the year. NLN, South West Breweries Limited, Annual Report, 1982.
[42] Wallace, M., *A History of Namibia: From the Beginning to 1990* (2011 Cape Town) 274.
[43] Wallace notes that the struggle for independence is not simply a polarisation between SWAPO and the South African administration. Much of the literature is, however, focused on this dialectic relationship. Wallace describes our understanding of the final decades of South African rule as "rudimentary" and points out that this topic is "an important one for future historical writing." M. Wallace, *A History of Namibia: From the Beginning to 1990* (2011 Cape Town) 273.
[44] Interview with Bernd Masche, 15th February 2016.
[45] D. Stevenson, "The Mysterious Demographics of Beer Drinking," in: G. Miescher, L. Rizzo and J. Silvester (eds.), *Posters in Action* (Basel 2009) 103–106; Interview with Don Stevenson, 5th February 2016.
[46] Interview with Bernd Masche, 22nd January 2016.

Fig. 32: The SWB trucks were made mine-proof during the guerrilla war for independence.

Right before independence the brewery encountered its greatest controversy yet, namely a tumultuous strike and a boycott. In the election year of 1989, a shop steward of the Namibia Food and Allied Workers Union (Nafau) was dismissed by SWB following alleged misconduct and the refusal of a disciplinary hearing. In response, 300 colleagues from the brewery (including a number of workers from two hotels and the butchery that were part of the Ohlthaver & List Group) went on strike for the first time. The company gave the strikers 24 hours to return to work — those who continued to strike thereafter were to be dismissed.[47] This caused a widespread controversy, leading the shebeen owners in the north, the Namibia Tavern Association, and the influential newspaper The Namibian to boycott the brewery.[48]

The strikers blocked the entrance with rocks and produced anti-SWB posters. The non-striking SWB employees responded by going out during the night with special "Night Action Teams" to place marketing posters over the strike posters.[49] The Hansa employees were not on strike, so the plant in Swakopmund was forced to increase its production to maximum capacity to make sure that the beer production was still meeting

---

[47] Chairman Werner List spoke of "an unlawful strike and a boycott by certain dealers in sympathy with the strikers." NLN, South West Breweries Limited, Annual Report, 1990.
[48] H. Jauch, 'Ghosts from the past', *The Villager*, 27th May 2012.
[49] Interview with Bernd Masche, 22nd January 2016; Interview with Bernd Masche, 15th February 2016.

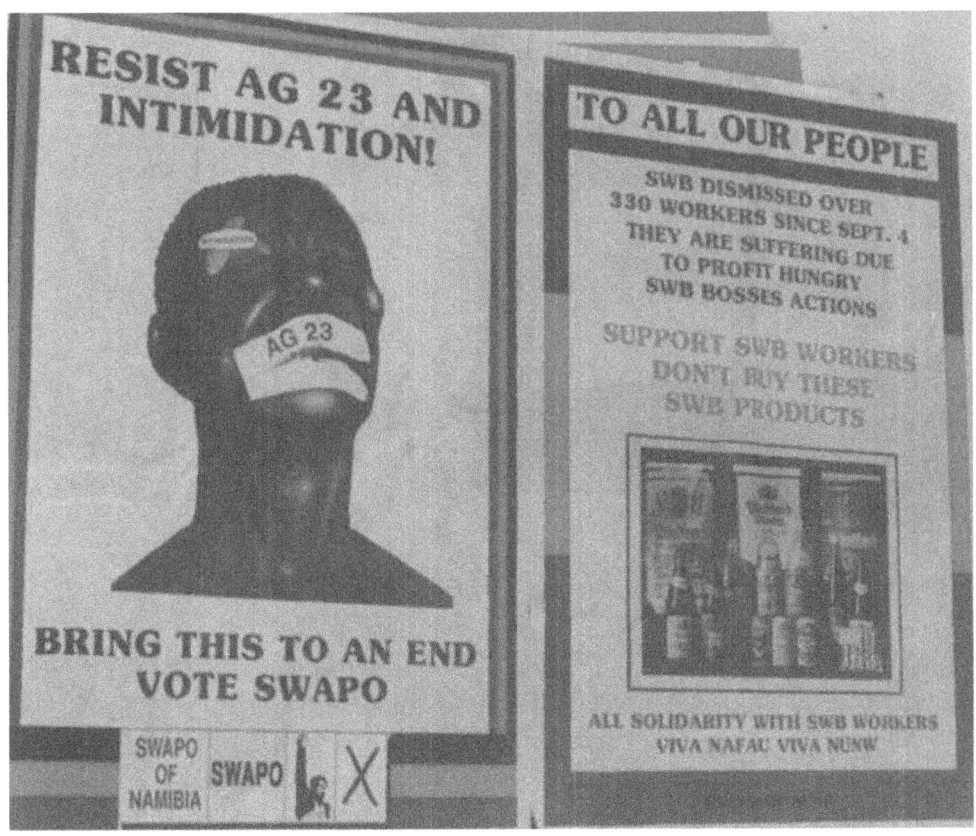

Fig. 33: Posters of the strike. During the night, SWB personnel covered these posters with beer advertisements.

the consumers' demands.[50] SWB and Nafau went to court and a settlement was reached in November 1989.[51]

The Namibian independence from South Africa was gained in 1990. SWB needed time to adjust to the new situation and the company continued under the name of South West Breweries for a little while, although this name was now outdated. On the label of the special independence lager, produced in honour of the Namibian freedom, one can still find the old company name — nothing on the bottle made it clear that a Namibian company was the producer.[52] Stevenson recalled that after independence the advertisement agency received a troubling phone call from a brewery manager. He explained that the newly ap-

---

[50] Interview Brenda Bravenboer with Helmut Pfaller, 26th May 2015.
[51] The problem, however, lingered on because some workers felt that they were not compensated properly. In 2012, a group of former SWB employees demonstrated outside the head office of Ohlthaver & List in response to the 1989 case. H. Jauch, 'Ghosts from the past', *The Villager*, 27th May 2012.
[52] NLN, Namibia Breweries Limited, Annual Report, 1991.

Fig. 34: Strikers laid rocks at the entrance of SWB.

pointed Namibian Minister of Trade and Industry received a tour around the plant and commented with surprise that he thought that SWB was a South African company.[53] It was clearly necessary to change the image of SWB and the new political situation was an opportunity to do so.

Once independence was a reality, the brewing company was transformed in a remarkable way. South West Breweries changed its name into Namibia Breweries and embraced its new Namibian identity. With a different name and a new identity for the company, the visual outlook of the company's marketing changed as well. The Reiterdenkmal image disappeared from the logo and was replaced by one that closely resembled the new Namibian flag. A new advertising campaign was launched to let the public know that the brewery was truly Namibian. The posters were published as a newspaper insert in order to reach a broader public.[54] Stevenson recalls:

> These advertisements informed the public that, not only was the Namibian Brewing industry locally owned and run, but that it provided employment for over 600 Namibians. The headlines of these ads proclaimed: "Whenever Namibians get together," "Brewed in Namibia by Namibians," "Spreading Good Cheer Throughout the Nation," "Brought to you by 600 Dedicated Namibians."[55]

---

[53] D. Stevenson, "The Mysterious Demographics of Beer Drinking," in: G. Miescher, L. Rizzo and J. Silvester (eds.), *Posters in Action* (Basel 2009) 103–106.
[54] Interview with Don Stevenson, 5th February 2016.
[55] D. Stevenson, "The Mysterious Demographics of Beer Drinking," in: G. Miescher, L. Rizzo and J. Silvester (eds.), *Posters in Action* (Basel 2009) 103–106.

Fig. 35: The special independence beer of South West Breweries.

Fig. 36: A poster of Namibia Breweries, published shortly after the Namibian independence.

Fig. 37: A poster of Namibia Breweries, shortly after Namibian independence.

Fig. 38: The first president of Namibia, Dr. Sam Nujoma (on the left) with Werner List (in the middle, with the tie), the chairman of NBL.

Most importantly, NBL put much effort in establishing a good and mutually beneficial relationship with the newly formed government. A powerful state-business alliance was the result. The brewers had an efficient lobby and effectively made clear to the government how important the brewery was for the Namibian economy. The brewing group had interests in basically all sectors of Namibian commerce and industry: hotels, supermarkets, a meat processor, livestock and dairy farms, fishing companies, real estate, and the list goes on.[56] In another publication, NBL claimed to directly and indirectly employ a staggering 1000 people, while paying NAD 12 million in tax annually and supporting various organisations.[57] Although the brewery vowed to adopt a neutral stance in the struggle for independence, the company had undeniable bargaining power in the political arena, as one of the largest private companies in a newly liberated country.

Simultaneously, the brewing company desperately needed the government's support. Proper liquor laws and protection against SAB were of foremost to NBL. Therefore, the

---

[56] NAN, F002-cp (in: JZ/0203) New sparkle for Namibian beer, 1985, Namibia Brief.
[57] NAN, F002-PC/0044, South West Breweries Breweries gazette.

interests of the new government and the market leader were mutual, and it helped that there was a good personal relationship between Sam Nujoma, the first President of Namibia and former SWAPO President, and Werner List, the chairman of NBL.[58] NBL employees were involved in the writing of the new liquor act and the beer industry was protected against SAB for the years to come.

In turn, NBL invested heavily in Namibia. The brewery was an important sponsor of athletic and cultural projects. They also sponsored projects such as "Smart Center" and "Development Trust Fund" which were used to finance other development projects. On one eventful occasion, when President Nujoma was celebrating his birthday, List donated six farms to the nation (meant for the University of Namibia) and NBL provided free beer at the party.[59] This shows the close relationship between the two entities.

The Beer War is Back

The newly organised NBL and its old nemesis SAB engaged in an energetic beer war from the 1990s onwards — this is the latest chapter in the development of the Namibian beer market. Both breweries now tried to build up a consumer base in each other's home country.[60] NBL aimed to grow its business in South Africa, while SAB wanted more market share in Namibia. The following section discusses the interests of both companies and gives a short history of the early trade relations between each brewery and the desired foreign market. Newspapers were filled with reports on the "beer war," which reminds us of the 1910s, when a fierce competition existed between the Felsenkellerbrauerei and the Kronenbrauerei and the newspapers were reporting on the "Bierkrieg."

South African Breweries

Let us first discuss SAB. For a considerable time, SAB yearned for a market share in Namibia, the home country of NBL. The size of SAB cannot be underestimated. At the end of the 20th century, SAB owned more than 90% of the southern African beer market —

---

[58] Interview with Hans Herrmann and Christian Müller, 18th November 2015; Interview with Bernd Masche, 22nd January 2016.

[59] R. Gordon, Inside the Windhoek Lager: Liquor and Lust in Namibia, in: W. Jankowiak and D. Bradburd (eds.) *Drugs, labor, and colonial expansion* (Tucson 2003) 121.

[60] It must be noted that import and export of beer has been happening for a long time. Perhaps one of the earliest examples occurred in 1905, when beers were moved from the Cape Colony into GSWA. The beverage company wrote to the administration in Cape Town that "We are not certain whether a permit is really necessary, to remove such Luxuries across the border." Roughly a century later, regulations were much stricter. WCARS, CO 8303, SA produce wine and brandy company: application for permit to send 10 tons of luxuries (beer etc) to German South West Africa via Ramonsdrift.

except Namibia. This enormous company had, in contrast to NBL, the advantage of the economies of scale: large breweries resulted in relatively low production costs.

South African beers had already been available in Namibia for roughly twenty-five years, although we are talking about small numbers of sales. The first South African beer brands in Namibia were Castle Lager and Lion Lager and they were distributed by SWB due to an agreement. However, the different philosophies between the two companies caused tension and the cooperation was aborted, as explained in the beginning of this chapter.[61]

Another way that South African beverages found their way to Namibia was through the South African Defence Force (SADF). SAB had an exclusive contract with the South African army to provide beers for the soldiers during the South African border war. Many South African troops resided in northern Namibia and Angola during this intense episode of the liberation struggle. As a result, northern Namibia experienced a vast influx of South African beer via SADF liquor outlets. The local economy even became dependent on beer. The drinking soldiers were "the backbone of the trade" in northern Namibia because a large percentage of their salaries was injected in the local economy through cuca shops.[62] Even teachers, farmers and civil servants established unlicensed bars to gain extra income.

The United Nations Transition Assistance Group (UNTAG) forces of the UN, sent to oversee the Namibian independence process, contributed to this development. The presence of soldiers influences not only the beer market, but also the economy in general, as we have already seen in the case of the First World War. To put the influence of SADF and UNTAG forces in perspective, let us consider an example. In the Oshakati-Ondangwa region in February 1990, a whopping 20% of the total amount of licensed traders dealt in alcohol. In addition to this staggering amount, a calculated 800 cuca shops were active in the region. The area was described as an "alcohol-driven economy," with an estimate of one cuca shop for every 100 people, excluding formal bars and private homes as places to drink beer.[63]

---

[61] Interview with Bogart Butler and Linda Buckingham, 17th February 2016.
[62] G. Dobler, *Traders and Trade in Colonial Ovamboland: Elite Formation and the Politics of Consumption under Indirect Rule and Apartheid, 1925–1990* (Basel 2014) 187. Dobler writes on the next page that beer consumption was officially legalised in 1973, but the new liquor legislation was already introduced in 1969. Furthermore, he discusses a company called "South West African Breweries," although it is not quite clear if he means South African Breweries or South West Breweries.
[63] Interview with Bogart Butler and Linda Buckingham, 17th February 2016; H. Siiskonen, 'Namibia and the Heritage of Colonial Alcohol Policy', *Nordic Journal of African Studies* Vol. 3 No. 1 (1994) 81; R. Gordon, Inside the Windhoek Lager: Liquor and Lust in Namibia, in: W. Jankowiak and D. Bradburd (eds.) *Drugs, labor, and colonial expansion* (Tucson 2003) 122-132.

In the early 1990s, SAB created Castle Brewing Namibia, a special company to bring their beers to Namibia. It started very small with only a few depots in large places such as Windhoek, the south as well as the north of Namibia. The ex-soldiers of the South West Africa Territorial Force (SWATF) and the South African expats that lived in Namibia formed the start of a consumer base for South African brews and formed the basis for the further expansion of SAB.[64]

Namibia Breweries

NBL was in desperate need to acquire a market share in South Africa, the home country of SAB. The reason for this is simple: Namibia is a small country with a very limited market in terms of customers. The SWB brewers needed to increase their production volume in order to survive the increasing economies of scale that characterises the global brewing industry. The key to this growth was, ironically, South Africa. This populous neighbouring country is rather close by: from the brewery in Windhoek it is only a distance of 1400 to 2000 kilometres to all major South African towns.[65] The local beer market in SWA was by far not strong enough to withstand the larger breweries of the world. SWB was already for a long time involved in the South African market, albeit on a small scale. German groups in Cape Town and Johannesburg formed an early consumers base.[66] Only after the transformation of SWB into NBL with a new brewery, distinctive products, an excise duty advantage, and its Namibian identity, the exporting of beer to South Africa really took off.

The Long Road to a SAB Brewery

Tension between the companies rose to a high level in the 1990s when SAB first attempted to build a brewery in northern Namibia.[67] This event showcases the strong alliance between NBL and the Namibian government, and sheds light on how a focus on "Namibian" beer became increasingly important for NBL to compete successfully with its South African rival. Since 1990, SAB tried to get a brewing license from the newly

---

[64] Interview with Bogart Butler and Linda Buckingham, 17th February 2016.
[65] Interview with Bernd Masche, 22nd January 2016. South Africa's population is far greater than that of other neighbours of Namibia. Furthermore, there were close historical ties between the two countries, with lots of traffic between them. Exporting to Angola would for example have been much more difficult because of the Angolan Civil War.
[66] Interview with Hans Herrmann and Christian Müller, 18th November 2015. Already in the early 1970s, SWB went to court with South African hotels because of payment issues. WCARS, CSC 2/1/1/3741, Illiquid case. Goods sold. South West Breweries Ltd. versus Murraysburg Hotel (Pty.) Ltd.; WCARS, 2/1/1/3744, Illiquid case. Goods sold. South West Breweries Ltd. versus Criterion Hotel.
[67] Interview with Bernd Masche, 22nd January 2016.

independent government.⁶⁸ SAB proposed to construct a NAD 100 million brewery in Ovamboland in 1994. The Namibian Trade and Industry Minister Hidepo Hamutenya gave it no chance of success, stating "We have a company (NBL) that is Namibian, that pays tax, and is the largest manufacturing plant employing over 8700 Namibians. We cannot let it be overrun by SAB."⁶⁹

The matter became a nationwide debate, covered in countless Namibian newspapers and magazines. In many ways, the discussion organised by the Namibia Economic Society in 2000 is an epitome of this debate. The Society claimed that hundreds of people from the government, corporations, and scholarly institutions came together to discuss "the controversy" of the beer industry in Namibia. Several speakers were present from both sides of the debate. NBL protested against the "imperialist drive" and "selfish, monopolistic ambitions" of SAB, threatening that an admission of SAB into Namibia would cause losses in jobs and tax incomes. SAB on the other hand argued for a free market and pointed out that black empowerment was a major part of the proposed SAB brewery.⁷⁰

Even so, the Namibian government rejected the request of SAB and continued to protect NBL. In return, NBL promised the government to build a small brewery in Tsumeb, named Tunweni. In this small plant, locally produced mahango was bought up to create a kind of sorghum beer, resembling the *oshikundu* beer that home brewers had been producing for centuries. The beer fermented inside milk cartons and had a shelf life of three days. The small brewery was not a success but ran for a few years. It proved to be difficult to transport the beer to all corners of Ovamboland due to the insufficient infrastructure in the region. Furthermore, bottle stores did not even want to obtain the cartons because they were afraid the cartons would leak and thus make their stores dirty. SAB maintained a similar operation in Johannesburg, South Africa, which was much more successful because the infrastructure was of sufficient quality. ⁷¹ This relationship is a fine example of the intimate ties between the state and industry, who understood that they needed each other. Through government protection, NBL had time to reinvent itself as a company and build up a strong export of beer to South Africa. In return, NBL invested in the development of Namibia.

---

[68] NLN, T16/0135, Namibia Economic Society Newsletter, Issue 19, March 2001; A. Mager, *Beer, Sociability and Masculinity in South Africa* (Bloomington 2010) 127.

[69] R. Gordon, Inside the Windhoek Lager: Liquor and Lust in Namibia, in: W. Jankowiak and D. Bradburd (eds.) *Drugs, labor, and colonial expansion* (Tucson 2003) 122.

[70] NLN, T16/0135, Namibia Economic Society Newsletter, Issue 19, March 2001: various articles.

[71] Interview with Bernd Masche, 22ⁿᵈ January 2016; Interview with Bernd Masche, 15ᵗʰ February 2016; Interview Brenda Bravenboer with Helmut Pfaller, 26ᵗʰ May 2015.

For many years, the Namibian government protected NBL, but new policies emerged with a new President (Nujoma stepped down after fifteen years of being President) and this proved to be an opportunity for SAB.[72] SAB had not given up on its dream of establishing a brewery in Namibia and kept requesting a brewing license from the national government. It took them ten years to acquire such a license in Namibia, but in the end the South African brewers managed to acquire such a permit in the early 2000s.

However, a new problem emerged: it was undecided which location would be acceptable to build the new SAB brewery on. After ten years of struggling to receive a brewing license, it took years to decide on a brewery location. Windhoek and Oshakati were favoured by SAB, but the government rejected both proposals. Finally, an agreement was reached for Okahandja. Then, it took years before SAB internally approved the final business case to actually build the plant.[73]

After twenty-five years of waiting, negotiating and planning, the desired SAB plant was operational in 2015.[74] According to SAB officials, the brewery in Okahandja was built on faith instead of economics because of the relatively small production volume. It was not immediately seen as a profitable business (only returnable quart bottles are produced in the brewery, all non-returnable packages are imported from South Africa). The reason that SAB still approved the project was partly because of the fact that NBL, together with Heineken, built a brewery in South Africa in 2011. "They built a brewery in our backyard," explains SAB manager Bogart Butler. The reason for the Okahandja plant was partly to irritate their Namibian competition. The advantage of this project is that costs of transporting beer from South Africa to Namibia are no longer necessary. The production started in September 2014 and the official launch was on the 1st July 2015. Three kinds of beers are produced (Carling Black Label, Castle Lite and Castle) and 135 people are employed.[75]

An Ongoing Rivalry

Besides the construction of breweries in each other's home countries, the beer battle was fought via a succession of creative marketing campaigns. Again, the "beer war" between NBL and SAB resembles the previous "beer war" of the 1910s between the Kronenbrauerei and the Felsenkellerbrauerei. The ongoing rivalry resulted in cheeky advertising and

---

[72] Interview with Hans Herrmann and Christian Müller, 18th November 2015.
[73] Interview with Bogart Butler and Linda Buckingham, 17th February 2016.
[74] The official launch was on the 15th July 2015, although the brewery was operational from September 2014 onwards. Interview with Bogart Butler and Linda Buckingham, 17th February 2016.
[75] Ibid.

a series of lawsuits. A whole book can be filled with stories on how these companies competed, but only three exemplary cases are selected for this publication: the Hofbräu incident, Windhoek's Lager advertisements, and the sewage rumour.[76]

From the 2000s onwards, NBL was doing exceptionally well in South Africa, enjoying an annually increasing export of beer.[77] Since NBL's unique selling point was the use of the Reinheitsgebot, SAB sought an answer in the launch of a new product with a distinct German heritage: a beer called Hofbräu. The plans for this brand were however leaked to the NBL management, a few weeks before the official launch by South African Breweries. NBL quickly responded by launching their own "Felsenkeller Hofbräu," filling the bottles with the already existing Tafel Lager and transporting it to South Africa prior to the launch of the regular Hofbräu.[78] The launch of the South African Hofbräu was thereby successfully undermined.

These tricks also worked the other way around. As many people know, Windhoek Lager is the flagship brand of NBL. SAB placed large billboards in the Namibian capital to promote their rivalling Castle beer — with the addition of an enormous tagline that said "Windhoek's Lager." The resemblance between Windhoek Lager and Windhoek's Lager cannot be missed. Another major Namibian brand is called Tafel Lager. SAB placed large billboards with the Afrikaans tagline: "Maak seker daar is 'n Castle op die tafel" [make sure there is a Castle on the table], again imitating the name of a famous Namibian beer. NBL went to court and won, meaning that SAB had to take these advertisements down. In response, SAB had new billboards placed around town with the text "You can't make great beer from sour grapes."[79]

Both companies accused each other of unprofessional behaviour and as a neutral spectator it is difficult to assess which stories are true and which ones are not. A fitting

---

[76] Another crucial incident was the controversy over the quarts bottle: while NBL and SAB quart bottles looked the same, NBL accused SAB of picking up their empty bottles at bottle stores and shebeens, so that NBL had to buy new ones. NBL spoke of "bullying tactics." NBL successfully went to the government for support, which made it more difficult for SAB to pursue this tactic. A Mager, *Beer, Sociability and Masculinity in South Africa* (Bloomington 2010) 126; R. Gordon, Inside the Windhoek Lager: Liquor and Lust in Namibia, in: W. Jankowiak and D. Bradburd (eds.) *Drugs, labor, and colonial expansion* (Tucson 2003) 121; Interview with Bernd Masche, 22nd January 2016.

[77] Already before independence, SWB was busy with new projects in South Africa, for instance with the launch of Windhoek Light in South Africa in 1984. Interview with Bernd Masche, 15th February 2016; Interview Brenda Bravenboer with Ernst Ender, 22nd May 2015.

[78] Interview with Bernd Masche, 15th February 2016. Mager writes down a different version of this event in her book on SAB. Basically, she turns the order of events around: SAB's Hofbräu was meant to fend off NBL's Hofbräu. Based on discussions with several NBL employees, another version has been put in this book. A. Mager, *Beer, Sociability and Masculinity in South Africa* (Bloomington 2010) 128.

[79] Interview with Bogart Butler and Linda Buckingham, 17th February 2016.

Fig. 39: The cheeky billboards of SAB.

example is the sewage beer rumour.[80] According to former NBL employees, SAB would hire people to go to shebeens, order a Namibian beer, and then theatrically spit the beer out on the ground while saying that it tasted like sewage, while adding that it was probably also made with sewage.[81] SAB officials refute this claim, but do explain that they applied a tactic called "wolfpacking": a large group of SAB people would to go a shebeen, to make sure that a major part of the crowd in that particular shebeen was SAB-minded. Then they would promote the SAB beers by ordering SAB drinks and talking to the other customers.[82] This is just one of the many examples of manipulation which each brewery accused the other of.

New Developments

Much happened in the Namibian beer industry during the last decade. NBL restructured itself in the O&L Group and found international partners to strengthen its brewing operation and enhance the global export of its product. An even stronger emphasis has been placed on the Namibian origin of its beer, exemplified through a new brand that is named "King Lager." King Lager has distinct local roots, as it is partly produced with Namibian grown barley, a project that is finally successful after years of experimenting and testing. Their modern advertisements consistently emphasise the "Namibianness" of NBL beers. Another trend, which is interwoven with the emphasis on Namibian roots, is the advent of new craft breweries.

In 2008, the Camelthorn Brewery opened its doors, meaning that the very first microbrewery of Namibia had started its brewing operations.[83] The founder is Jörg Finkeldey, a former chemical engineer of NBL. Camelthorn Brewery was the first local competitor of NBL since Hansa Brewery opened up roughly 80 years ago. The first beers were launched in 2009 and in six months' time, five different brands were launched. Unfortunately, the brewery soon had trouble surviving. The beer market in Namibia was still quite small. It is dominated by NBL and craft beer was a relatively new phenomenon back then. In 2012, negotiations with NBL started whether Camelthorn should be liquidated or bought up by NBL. In the end, NBL decided to buy up Camelthorn Brewery, including the brand and the equipment. The Camelthorn Weissbeer brand was kept by NBL and is still being

---

[80] R. Gordon, Inside the Windhoek Lager: Liquor and Lust in Namibia, in: W. Jankowiak and D. Bradburd (eds.) *Drugs, labor, and colonial expansion* (Tucson 2003) 122.
[81] Masche is just one who circulates this rumour: Interview with Bernd Masche, 22nd January 2016.
[82] Interview with Bogart Butler and Linda Buckingham, 17th February 2016.
[83] B. Hesse, 'Africa's Intoxicating Beer Markets', *African Studies Review* Vol. 58, No. 1 (2015) 105.

brewed today, because it resonated with the German Namibian market.[84] Today it is marketed as a distinctly Namibian craft beer.

In 2015, the first pub brewery in Namibia opened its doors: the Swakopmund Brewing Company (SBC). The small brewery is part of the Strand Hotel, owned by the O&L Group. The SBC is meant as a place for the NBL brewers to experiment and brew beers different from the regular NBL range. Three kinds of beers are available at any time; all of them are specifically brewed for the SABC and follow the regulations of the Reinheitsgebot. The brewery does not yet sell bottled beers because their liquor license does not allow it. Roughly 1000 litres of beer are produced per week, while the maximum capacity is 2000 litres.[85] The SBC is meant to be different from NBL. The brewery is supported, for instance, with the supply of ingredients and NBL ensures the quality control. The master brewer of SBC is employed by NBL but remains quite independent.[86]

While both the Camelthorn Brewery and the SBC are currently part of NBL, and can therefore not really be considered competition, two new breweries were founded in recent years: The Skeleton Coast Brewery and the Namib Dunes Craft Brewery. Both are located along Namibia's coastline. It is a clear sign that the craft brewing culture is developing in Namibia and shows the importance of a local origin of beer.

In conclusion, SWB reinvented itself due to the threat of a foreign competitor and a series of historical events that were used to its advantage. In the 1970s, SWB became synonymous with the national beer industry. There was virtually no other domestic competitor and the black population was finally legally allowed to drink liquor. However, the fact that SWB were unable to distribute their beer among the more densely populated northern Namibia was an obstacle. At the time, SWB was completely focused on the white settler community, because of its particular history as a company.

The desire of SWB to set foot in SWA was highly problematic and forced SWB to reinvent itself. The opening up of the northern part of Namibia gave SWB momentum. What followed was a new and professional brewery, a new strategy that embraced the Reinheitsgebot and a new image due to Namibian independence. This changed SWB into NBL. A powerful alliance with the newly elected government ensured protection against SAB so that the brewery could grow and look for export markets.

---

[84] Interview with Jörg Finkeldey, 12th February 2016.
[85] Interview with Stephan Koepp, 8th February 2016.
[86] Interview with Hans Herrmann and Christian Müller, 18th November 2015.

Conclusion

Beer is a compelling subject of scholarship for African Studies because it allows us a window into business-state relations, specifically when it concerns the contentious issue of nationalism. To understand the enigma of how beer was transformed from a settlers' icon to the symbol of an independent Namibian nation, it is vital to look at the deeper history of the beer market. The Namibian beer market and the historical events that shaped the south-western part of Africa are closely interwoven. As discussed, beer brewing existed for hundreds of years before the first European explorers arrived. When GSWA was established at the end of the 19th century, foreign settlers flocked to the newly established Protectorate. In the early days of the German colony, settler communities imported beers from Europe on a large scale, but in the early 20th century numerous small breweries popped up all over the Protectorate.

The local commercial brewing industry mainly thrived in the towns of Swakopmund, Windhoek and Omaruru, the so-called 'beer triangle.' After World War I it became increasingly difficult to maintain brewing operations. Competition was fierce, leading to a 'beer war' amongst local breweries in the territory. In 1920, SWB was founded by merging the largest breweries of the country into a single company. During the occupation of South Africa, beer became a pivotal instrument in apartheid politics. The commercial beer market consisted of white settlers only, who hailed the brews of SWB as their national drink. Their beer became a symbol of their cultural identity. After decades of a problematic divide between a white market and a black market, the prohibitive legislation was repealed in 1969 and the African population was legally allowed to consume beer.

In the meantime, SWB faced serious competition from SAB, a foreign competitor that owned more than 90% of the southern African beer market and desired to expand its business into SWA. SWB had to reinvent itself as a company and needed a new strategy. A series of historical events were utilised to the advantage of the brewing company. One major event was the opening up of Ovamboland in the 1970s, the northern part of SWA where the majority of the population lived. When SWB was able to connect with this consumer base, a surge in sales was the result.

With the opening up of Ovamboland, the northern part of SWA became part of the national beer market. Half of the population was now connected with the commercial beer market that had emerged from the centre of the country. A new brewing plant was needed to accommodate the steep development of SWB. The construction of a new plant allowed for a change of brewing practices: SWB introduced the German Reinheitsgebot, a centuries old set of purity laws, for the production of its beer in the 1980s. Following the Namibian independence of 1990, South West Breweries quickly changed into Namibia Breweries and embraced the new Namibia.

NBL cleverly made an unofficial alliance with the Namibian government. A coalition between the state elite and the brewery management made it possible to win over black customers, to export its beer to overseas countries, and to protect the national industry from SAB for 25 years. Approaching Namibian nationalism from the perspective of the beer market provides an unparalleled view of the volatile nature of (political) identity, as it shows how a single economic product can be coupled with diametrically opposed identities.

Over the course of a century, and despite difficult political and economic conditions, NBL and its predecessor were able to brew beer. This book places much emphasis on the brewers throughout Namibian history: home brewers were able to make beer already centuries before the arrival of Europeans, the first settlers managed to start brewing companies in a strange environment and the brewers of SWB/NBL kept their operations going despite many obstacles. Drawing on a rich archive of sources, ranging from colonial letters to beer bottles, this study shows the chameleon character of beer. Once a relic of colonial times, Namibian beer is now widely celebrated as one of the best known examples of Namibian nationalism. It is a surprising history that says volumes about the ways businesses and states interact.

Abbreviations

A.G.	Aktiengesellschaft. German for *Incorporated Company* (Inc.)
G.m.b.H.	Gesellschaft mit beschränkter Haftung. German for *Limited Company* (Ltd.)
GSWA	German South West Africa
Nafau	Namibia Food and Allied Workers Union
NAN	National Archives of Namibia
NBL	Namibia Breweries Limited
NLN	National Library of Namibia
NSE	Namibia Economic Society
NSS	Namibia Scientific Society
O&L	Ohlthaver & List
SAB	South African Breweries
SADF	South African Defence Force
SBC	Swakopmund Brewing Company
SSS	Scientific Society Swakopmund
SWA	South West Africa
SWAPO	South West Africa People's Organisation
SWB	South West Breweries
UN	United Nations
UNTAG	United Nations Transition Assistance Group
WCARS	Western Cape Archives and Records Service

List of figures

1. Perry-Castañeda Library Map Collection.
2. National Archives of Namibia, no. 13796.
3. Swakopmund Museum, photo by Tycho van der Hoog.
4. From the collection of Mannfred Goldbeck.
5. National Archives of Namibia, no. 01407.
6. This map is kindly produced by Snowballstudio.
7. Tise map is kindly produced by Snowballstudio.
8. Scientific Society Swakopmund, no. 2004.19.59, photo by Tycho van der Hoog.
9. Scientific Society Swakopmund, no. A 0EE 5857.
10. Namibia Scientific Society, no. 5124/24/FA20.
11. From the collection of Brigitte Schunemann.
12. National Archives of Namibia, 01921.
13. From the collection of Gunter von Schumann.
14. Brauhaus Swakopmund, photo by Tycho van der Hoog.
15. Swakopmund Scientific Society, no. 2004.31.28, photo by Tycho van der Hoog.
16. From the collection of Lothar Geier.
17. Namibia Breweries Limited.
18. From the collection of Brenda Bravenboer.
19. National Archives of Namibia, no. 12606.
20. Scientific Society Swakopmund, no. 2009.20.54
21. Namibia Breweries Limited.
22. Namibia Breweries Limited.
23. National Archives of Namibia, no. 03196.
24. National Archives of Namibia, no. 24558.
25. From the collection of Mannfred Goldbeck.
26. Swakopmund Museum, photo by Snowballstudio.
27. From the collection of Gunter von Schumann.
28. From the collection of Don Stevenson.
29. From the collection of Don Stevenson, photo by Snowballstudio.
30. From the collection of Bernd Masche.
31. Namibia Breweries Limited.
32. From the collection of Bernd Masche.
33. From the collection of Bernd Masche.
34. From the collection of Bernd Masche.
35. From the collection of Don Stevenson, photo by Snowballstudio.
36. From the collection of Don Stevenson.
37. From the collection of Don Stevenson.
38. From the collection of Bernd Masche.
39. From the collection of Linda Buckingham.

Bibliography

Archival Material

National Archives of Namibia

NAN, ADM 120, Plans. Felsenkeller Brauerei. New Building.

NAN, ADM 121, Plans. Felsenkeller Brauerei. New Building.

NAN, ADM 122, Plans. Felsenkeller Brauerei. Shed.

NAN, ADM 123, Building Plan. Felsenkeller Brewery. Tal Street. Additions: Beer Cooling Room. Plot 142/35 Section 4.

NAN, ADM 127, Breweries: Felsenkeller Brauerei establishment of a brewery at Omaruru.

NAN, ADM 217, Claims: Felsenkeller Brauerei.

NAN, ADM 244, Claims: Felsenkeller Brauerei.

NAN, BWI 184, Grunderwerb. Felsenkeller Brauerei (Vormals Karl Bauer und Kretzschmann).

NAN, BWI 428 Getränkeanmeldungen der Felsenkellerbrauerei.

NAN, COM 17, The Union Brewery Limited (Private Company): Registrations.

NAN, COM 17, The Union Brewery Limited (Private Company): Returns.

NAN, F002-AA/1996, The liquor law of South-West Africa: being the Liquor Licensing Proclamation, 1920 (Proclamation no.6 of 1920), as amended from time to time, with notes, references to decided casses [sic] and other relevant legislation.

NAN, F002-cp (in: JZ/0203) New sparkle for Namibian beer, 1985, Namibia Brief.

NAN, F002-cp, H. Heuschneider, Kleine Chronik der Hansa-Brauerei 2005.

NAN, F002-JX/0195, Bericht der Felsenkeller Brauerei Aktiengesellschaft 1912.

NAN, F002-L.0781a, Commission of Enquiry: Sale of liquor and desecration of Sunday.

NAN, F002-NAMZ 0528, Andreas Vogt, Wine, beer and song in hotels of old Windhoek, Informanté, 2006.

NAN, F002-NAMZ 0559, J. Silvester, A trail of broken beer bottles, the Namibian Weekender, 10/09/99.

NAN, F002-PA/0110, The liquor law of the South-West Africa Protectorate.

NAN, F002-PA/0120, Memorandum and articles of the South West Breweries Limited 1920.

NAN, F002-PC/0044, South West Breweries Breweries gazette.

NAN, F002-RARA/062, Native beverages 1931.

NAN, Grundstück Omaruru. Parzelle 11 Blatt 3. Besitzer Bauer (Felsenkellerbrauerei Windhoek).

NAN, HRW 10, Handelsregistersache. Felsenkellerbrauerei.

NAN, HRW 9, Handelsregistersache. Felsenkellerbrauerei Windhuk.

NAN, JUS 156, Kaffir beer.

NAN, MOK 1/2/1, Felsenkellerbrauerei, Parzelle 36, Blatt 5.

NAN, MTS 8, Non-European Affairs: Beer Hall.

NAN, NAO 071, Native Customs and Practices, Distilling Alcohol.

NAN, NAO 071, Native Customs and Practices, Distilling Alcohol.

NAN, SWAA 150, Ovamboland. Distilling of alcohol by natives.

NAN, SWAA 1504, Ovamboland. Distilling of alcohol by natives.

NAN, SWAA 2569, Trading with the enemy. The South West Africa Breweries.

NAN, SWAA 2572, Trading with the enemy. Hansa Breweries, Swakopmund.

NAN, SWAA 3113, Customs and Excise: Brewery Regulations.

NAN, SWAA 3113, Customs and Excise: Brewery regulations.

NAN, SWAA 3115, Monthly Revenu [sic] Returns: Alleged customs fraud Hansa Brewery Swakopmund.

National Library of Namibia

NLN, 96/0511 B, Namibia Breweries Limited, 1920–1995.

NLN, T16/0135, Namibia Economic Society Newsletter, Issue 19, March 2001.

NLN, South West Breweries Limited, Annual Report, 1924–1925.

NLN, South West Breweries Limited, Annual Report, 1979.

NLN, South West Breweries Limited, Annual Report, 1981.

NLN, South West Breweries Limited, Annual Report, 1982.

NLN, South West Breweries Limited, Annual Report, 1990.

NLN, Namibia Breweries Limited, Annual Report, 1991.

Namibia Scientific Society

NSS, Annual Report of the Windhoek Chamber of Commerce, 29th November 1920 – 31st March 1922.

NSS, Bourquin, A., Omaruru: Die Geschichte einer Stadt (unpublished, 1969).

NSS, Brewing Excellence since 1920, Namibian, 21/06/99.

NSS, Das Brennglas, No. 1, Jahrg. 1920.

NSS, Fitzner, R., Adressbuch für Deutsch-Südwestafrika 1908 (Berlin 1908).

NSS, Flamingo, Air Namibia in-flight magazine, May 2012.

NSS, Jahresbericht der Windhuker Handelskammer 1912.

NSS, Jahresbericht der Windhuker Handelskammer 1913.

NSS, Jahresbericht der Windhuker Handelskammer, 1910–1911.

NSS, Jahresbericht der Windhuker Handelskammer, 1911–1912.

NSS, Peters, W., Baukunst in Südwestafrika 1884–1914 (Windhoek 1981).

NSS, Report of Chamber of Commerce, Windhoek, 1923–1924

NSS, South West Africa Annual, 1953 / Suidwes-Afrika-Jaarboek, 1953.

NSS, Südwestafrikanisches Adressenbuch 1921.22 / Directory of South West Africa.

NSS, Territory of South West Africa, Report on the Census of the European Population, taken on the 4th May, 1926.

NSS, Territory of South-West Africa, Report on the Census of the European Population, taken on the 3rd May, 1921.

NSS, Van ossewa tot besige sakesentrum in stad, Republikein, 30/10/97.

NSS, Vedder, H., 'Notes on the Brewing of Kaffir Beer in S.W.A.: A History of Beer', Journal of the South West Africa Scientific Society, Vol. 3 (1951) 41–43.

Scientific Society Swakopmund

SSS, 2000.1.1013, Der Bierkrieg 1916.

SSS, 2000.1.702, Hundert Jahre Südwestafrika.

SSS, 2000.1.860, Geschäfts-Eröffnung.

SSS, 2000.1.861, Bericht der Felsenkellerbrauerei Aktiengesellschaft.

SSS, 2000.1.907, Erweiterung der Kronen-Brauerei.

SSS, 2004.115.2, Rechnung der Brauerei Hanke in Karibib und Herr Hier.

SSS, 2004.115.26, Brewery Historical Information – How it was established in Keetmanshoop.

SSS, 2004.19.33, Gründung der ersten Brauerei 1912, Felsenkeller-Brauerei in Windhoek.

SSS, 2004.19.59, Anzeigen: Ein guter Spiegel der damaligen Wirtschaftslage.

SSS, 2004.31.28, Zur Feier der Eröffnung der Kronen-Brauerei in Windhoek.

SSS, 2004.9.17, Ein Teil Südwester Zeitgeschehens.

SSS, Hansa-Brauerei Limited Swakopmund, 7. Geschäftsjahr 1935–1936 (uncatalogued).

SSS, Hansa-Brauerei Limited Swakopmund, 8. Geschäftsjahr 1936–1937 (uncatalogued).

SSS, Memorandum und Statuten der Hansa Brauerei Limited (uncatalogued).

SSS, Pesch, L. and G. Murray, Omaruru: Im Laufe der Zeit (no publishing information).

Western Cape Archives and Records Services

WCARS, 2/1/1/3744, Illiquid case. Goods sold. South West Breweries Ltd. versus Criterion Hotel.

WCARS, 3/CT, 4/1/9/1/137, Liquor. Proposed establishment of bantu beer brewery (also tour of up country establishments re same). [sic]

WCARS, CMT 3/1086, Liquor: kaffir beer. General.

WCARS, CO 8303, SA produce wine and brandy company: application for permit to send 10 tons of luxuries (beer etc) to German South West Africa via Ramonsdrift.

WCARS, CSC 2/1/1/3741, Illiquid case. Goods sold. South West Breweries Ltd. versus Murraysburg Hotel (Pty.) Ltd.

WCARS, GH 1/460, Papers received from Secretary of State, London: general dispatches. The liquor traffic in the German protectorate in South West Africa.

Interviews

Interview with Hans Herrmann and Christian Müller, supply chain manager and master brewer Namibia Breweries, 18th November 2015.

Interview with Bernd Masche, former managing director of Namibia Breweries, 22nd January 2016.

Interview with Lothar Geier, grandson of SWB brewer Julius Geier, 26th January 2016.

Interview with Bernd Masche, former managing director of Namibia Breweries, 27th January 2016.

Interview with Brigitte Schünemann, granddaughter of brewer Friedrich Schmidt, 4th February 2016.

Interview with Don Stevenson, former advertising director Adfactory, 5th February 2016.

Interview with Stephan Koepp, master brewer of Swakopmund Brewing Company 8th February 2016.

Interview with Jörg Finkeldey, founder of Camelthorn Brewery, 12th February 2016.

Interview with Bernd Masche, former managing director of Namibia Breweries, 15th February 2016.

Interview with Bogart Butler and Linda Buckingham, technical manager and national trade marketing manager at SABMiller Namibia, 17th February 2016.

Interview with Lothar Geier, grandson of SWB brewer Julius Geier, 18th February 2016.

Interview with Gunter von Schumann, former resident of Omaruru, 18th February 2016.

Interview Brenda Bravenboer with Ernst Heuschneider, former manager at Hansa Brewery, 27th February 2012.

Interview Brenda Bravenboer with Helmut Pfaller, former master brewer of Namibia Breweries, 26th May 2015.

Interview Brenda Bravenboer with Ernst Ender, former marketing manager of Namibia Breweries 22nd May 2015.

Literature

Albertyn, A.P.J., *Die Ensiklopedie Van Name In Suidwes-Afrika* (Pretoria 1984).

Baines, T., *Explorations in South West Africa* (London 1864).

Bravenboer, B., *Windhoek: Capital of Namibia* (Windhoek 2004).

Bryceson, D. (ed.), *Alcohol in Africa: Mixing Business, Pleasure, and Politics* (Portsmouth 2002).

Chabal, P., and N. Vidal (eds.), *Angola: the weight of history* (London 2007).

Curto, J.C., 'Alcohol in Africa: a preliminary compilation of the post-1875 literature', *A Current Bibliography on African Affairs*, Vol. 21 No. 1 (1989) 3–31.

de Garine, I. and V. de Garine (eds.), *Drinking: Anthropological Approaches* (New York 2001).

Dewitz, C. von, *Swakopmund: Der kleine Stadtführer* (Windhoek 2009).

---, *Windhoek: A brief city guide* (Windhoek 2009).

Dietler, M., 'Alcohol: Anthropological/Archaeological Perspectives', *Annual Review of Anthropology* Vol. 35 (2006) 229–249.

Dobler, G., 'License to Drink. Between Liberation and Inebriation in Northern Namibia', in: S. van Wolputte and M. Fumanti (eds.), *Beer in Africa: Drinking Spaces, States and Selves* (Münster 2010) 167–191.

---, *Traders and Trade in Colonial Ovamboland: Elite Formation and the Politics of Consumption under Indirect Rule and Apartheid, 1925–1990* (Basel 2014).

Douglas, M. (ed.), *Constructive Drinking: Perspectives on Drink from Anthropology* (Cambridge 1987).

Embashu, W. et al., 'Processing methods of Oshikundu, a traditional beverage from subtribes within Aawambo culture in the Northern Namibia', *Journal for Studies in Humanities and Social Sciences* Vol. 2 No. 1 (2013) 117–127.

Embashu, W., A. Cheikhyoussef, G. Kahaka, *Survey on Indigenous Knowledge and Household processing methods of Oshikundu; a cereal-based fermented beverage from Oshana, Oshikoto, Ohangwena and Omusati Regions in Namibia*, Multidisciplinary Research Centre, University of Namibia (Windhoek 2012).

Erichsen, C.W., *"The angel of death has descended violently among them" Concentration camps and prisoners of-war in Namibia, 1904–08* (Leiden 2005).

Fage, J.D., *A History of Africa* (London 1988).

Forbes, V., *Anders Sparrman Travels in the Cape 1772–76* (Cape Town 1975).

---, *Travels and Adventures in Southern Africa by George Thompson* (Cape Town 1968).

Freyer, E.P.W., *Chronik von Otavi und Umgebung 1906–1966* (Windhoek 1966).

Fumanti, M., '"I Like My Windhoek Lager": Beer Consumption and the Making of Men in Namibia', in: S. van Wolputte and M. Fumanti (eds.), *Beer in Africa: Drinking Spaces, States and Selves* (Münster 2010) 257–274.

Gewald, J.B., 'Diluting Drinks and Deepening Discontent: Colonial Liquor Controls and Public Resistance in Windhoek, Namibia', in: D. Bryceson (eds.), *Alcohol in Africa: Mixing Business, Pleasure, and Politics* (Portsmouth 2002) 117–138.

---, *Herero Heroes: A Socio-Political History of the Herero of Namibia 1890–1923* (Oxford 1999).

Gordon, R., 'The Impact of the Second World War on Namibia', *Journal of Southern African Studies* Vol. 19, No. 1 (1993) 147–165.

---, Inside the Windhoek Lager: Liquor and Lust in Namibia, in: W. Jankowiak and D. Bradburd (eds.) *Drugs, labor, and colonial expansion* (Tucson 2003) 117–134.

Grotpeter, J.J. *Historical Dictionary of Namibia* (Metuchen 1994).

Haggblade, S., 'The Shebeen Queen and the Evolution of Botswana's Sorghum Beer Industry', in: J. Crush and C Ambler (eds.), *Liquor and Labor in Southern Africa* (Athens 1992) 395–412.

Hahn, H., 'Consumption, Identities and Agency in Africa: Introduction', in: H. Hahn (ed.), *Consumption in Africa: Anthropological Approaches* (Berlin 2008) 9–42.

Hansen, T.B. and F. Stepputat, 'Sovereignty Revisited', *Annual Review of Anthropology* Vol. 35 (2006) 295–315.

Hartmann, W., J. Silvester and P. Hayes (eds.), *The colonising camera: Photographs in the making of Namibian History* (Cape Town 1998).

Hayes, P. et al., *Namibia under South African Rule: Mobility and Containment 1915–46* (Oxford 1988).

Heap, S., 'Alcohol in Africa: a supplementary list of post-1875 literature', *A Current Bibliography on African Affairs* Vol. 26 No. 1 (1994) 1–14.

Henno, M., *Wenn es Krieg gibt, gehen wir in die Wüste* (Windhoek 1970).

Herre, H., 'Erinnerungen an die Lagerzeit in Andalusia', in: R. Kock (ed.), *Erinnerungen an die Internierungszeit (1939–1946) und zeitgeschichtliche Ergänzungen* (Windhoek 2003) 51–108.

Hesse, B., 'Africa's Intoxicating Beer Markets', *African Studies Review* Vol. 58, No. 1 (2015) 91–111.

Heyns, P. et al., *Namibia's Water, A Decision Makers' Guide* (Windhoek 1998).

Jäschke, U. and B. Bravenboer (eds.), *History of the Namibian road sector* (Windhoek 2011).

Kangumu, B., *Contesting Caprivi: A History of Colonial Isolation and Regional Nationalism in Namibia* (Basel 2011).

L'ange, G., *Urgent Imperial Service: South African Forces in German South West Africa 1914–1915* (Cape Town 1991).

Lastovia, E. and A. Lastovia, *Bottles & Bygones* (Cape Town 1982).

Lau, B. and C. Sterk, *Namibian Water Resources and their Management: A Preliminary History*, ARCHEIA No. 15 (Windhoek 1990).

Lightfoot, E., M. Maree and J. Ananias, 'Exploring the relationship between HIV and alcohol use in a remote Namibian mining community', *African Journal of AIDS Research* Vol. 8 No. 3 (2009) 321–327.

Luning, S., 'To drink or not to drink: beer brewing, rituals, and religious conversion in Maane, Burkina Faso', in: D. Bryceson, *Alcohol in Africa: mixing business, pleasure, and politics* (Portsmouth 2002) 321–248.

Mager, A., 'One Beer, "One Goal, One Nation, One Soul": South African Breweries, Heritage, Masculinity and Nationalism, 1960–1999', *Past and Present* Vol. 188 (2005) 163–194.

---, 'The First Decade of 'European Beer' in Apartheid South Africa: The State, the Brewers and the Drinking Public, 1962–72', *The Journal of African History* Vol. 40 No. 3 (1999) 367–388.

---, 'White Liquor Hits Black Livers: Meanings of Excessive Liquor Consumption in South Africa in the Second Half of the Twentieth Century', *Social Science and Medicine* Vol. 59 (2004) 735–751.

---, *Beer, Sociability and Masculinity in South Africa* (Bloomington 2010).

Mandelbaum, D.G., 'Alcohol and Culture', *Current Anthropology* Vol 6. No. 3 (1965) 281–293.

McGregor, G., and M. Goldbeck, *The First World War in Namibia: August 1914 – July 1915 (*Windhoek 2014).

Miescher, G., L. Rizzo and J. Silvester (eds.), *Posters in Action* (Basel 2009).

Otto, A. and G. von Schumann, Hoofstraat Omaruru (unpublished, 1986).

Pan, L., *Alcohol in Colonial Africa* (Helsinki 1975).

Pattman, R., '"The Beer Drinkers Say I Had a Nice Prostitute, but the Churchgoers Talk about Things Spiritual": Learning to be Men at Teacher's College in Zimbabwe', in: R. Morrell (ed.), *Changing Men in Southern Africa* (Scottsville 2001) 225–238.

Pomuti, A., and G. Eiseb, 'Alcohol abuse: a southern Namibian survey' Windhoek: Namibian Institute for Social and Economic Research (1990).

Porter, J.R., 'Antony van Leeuwenhoek: Tercentenary of His Discovery of Bacteria', *Bacteriological Reviews* Vol. 40 No. 2 (1976) 260–269.

Rautenberg, H., *Das alte Swakopmund: 1892–1919* (Swakopmund 1967).

Rodin, R.J., *The Ethnobotany of the Kwanyama Ovambos* (Lawrence 1985).

Rose, A.H. and J.S. Harrison (eds.), *The Yeasts: Yeast Technology (London 1993).*

Rosenthal, E., *Tankards & Tradition* (Cape Town 1961).

Rudner, I. and J. Rudner, *Axel Wilhelm Eriksson of Hereroland (1846–1901): His Life and Letters* (Windhoek 2006).

Schumann, G. von, and G. McGregor, *The Equestrian Monument (Reiterdenkmal) 1912–2014: A chronological documentation of reports, newspaper clippings and photos/illustrations* (Windhoek 2014).

Scientific Society Swakopmund, *Swakopmund: Eine kleine Chronik* (Swakopmund 2006).

Siiskonen, H., 'Namibia and the Heritage of Colonial Alcohol Policy', *Nordic Journal of African Studies* Vol. 3 No. 1 (1994) 77–86.

Silvester, J. and J.B. Gewald (eds.), *Words Cannot Be Found. German Colonial Rule in Namibia: An Annotated Report of the 1918 Blue Book* (Leiden 2003).

Stevenson, D., "The Mysterious Demographics of Beer Drinking," in: G. Miescher, L. Rizzo and J. Silvester (eds.), *Posters in Action* (Basel 2009) 103–106.

Steyn, W.K. (ed.), *100 Jare – Years – Jahre Keetmanshoop* (1966).

Tönjes, H., *Ovamboland* (Windhoek 1996).

United Nations Development Programme, 'Alcohol and human development in Namibia, *Namibia human development report* (1999).

van der Hoog, T.A., Brewing Identity: Beer and the Establishment of the Namibian Nation (unpublished MA thesis, 2016), Leiden University, Leiden.

Vansina, J., *Oral Tradition as History* (Suffolk 1985).

Vedder, H., *Das alte Südwestafrika: Die Geschichte Südwestafrikas bis zum Tode Maharero 1890* (Berlin reprint 1985).

Wallace, M., *A History of Namibia: From the Beginning to 1990* (Cape Town 2011).

Waterhouse, H., *Simon van der Stel's Journal of his Expedition to Namaqualand, 1685–6* (London 1932).

Williams, F.N., *Precolonial Communities of Southwestern Africa: A History of Owambo Kingdoms 1600–1920* (Windhoek 1991).

Wolputte, S. van, 'Beers and Bullets, Beads and Bulls. Drink and the Making of Margins in a Small Namibian

Towns', in: S. van Wolputte and M. Fumanti (eds.), *Beer in Africa: Drinking Spaces, States and Selves* (Münster 2010) 79–105.

Wolputte, S. van, and M. Fumanti (eds.), *Beer in Africa: Drinking Spaces, States and Selves* (Münster 2010).

Zappa, F., with P. Occhiogrosso, 'America Drinks & Goes Marching', in: F. Zappa with P. Occhiogrosso, *The Real Frank Zappa Book* (New York 1999).

Zeller, J., 'Symbol politics: Notes on the German colonial culture of remembrance', in: J. Zimmerer and J. Zeller, *Genocide in German South-West Africa: The Colonial War of 1904–1908 And Its Aftermath* (Berlin 2003) 231–251.

Zuern, E., 'Memorial politics: challenging the dominant party's narrative in Namibia', *The Journal of Modern African Studies* Vol. 40 No. 03 (2012) 493-518.

Websites

Hansa Pilsener History <http://hansapilsener.co.za/the-beer/history> (accessed on 21st May 2016).

SABMiller History, <http://ursus-breweries.ro/sabmiller-in-lume/istoric/?lng=2> (accessed on 5th July 2016).

World Population Review, <http://worldpopulationreview.com/countries/namibia-population> (accessed on 17th April 2019).

Newspapers

Tjirera, E., 'Dried peas and the politics of inebriation', *Insight Namibia*, December 2015 – January 2016.

Menges, W., 'Native? Sorry, no dried peas', *The Namibian*, 22nd August 2014.

Landes-Zeitung für Südwestafrika, 28th April 1923.

Jauch, H., 'Ghosts from the past', *The Villager*, 17th May 2012.

Schumann, G. von, 'Windhoek: a place of many names in the past', *NamPost*, March 1995, 22–23.

Appendix 1: Overview of Breweries

Over the years, an impressive number of breweries existed and continue to exist in Namibia. Most (historical) companies remain shrouded in mystery, as their records are scarce and scattered over various places. After months of archival research and interviews, a number of breweries could be identified. Below, a first attempt is made to give an overview of the numerous brewing companies that were founded on Namibian soil. The list is not comprehensive and future research will possibly reveal more breweries and their background stories. The author welcomes new information concerning this overview.

Name	Place	Time	Director	Known brands
Swakopmunder Brauerei	Swakopmund	Founded in 1900, now closed	Rudolph Jauch	Bavaria Bräu
Schmidt Brauerei	Klein Windhoek	Founded in 1902, now closed	Friedrich Schmidt	–
Felsenkellerbrauerei	Windhoek	Founded in 1902, now closed	Karl Bauer, Richard Kretschmann, Johann Heuschneider, Leopold Mahler, Frits Hummels, Peter Müller	Windhoek Urquell
Brauerei Grootfontein	Grootfontein	–	–	–
Bierbrauerei und Selterwasserfabrik	Karibib	Active around 1908, now closed	H. Kahl	–
Brauerei	Okahandja	Active around 1908, now closed	C. Bauer	–
Brauerei	Rehoboth	Active around 1908, now closed	Breckwoldt & Müller	–
Brauerei	Lüderitzbucht	Active around 1908, now closed	Johannes Osbahr	–
Brauerei	Keetmanshoop	Active around 1908, now closed	Johannes Osbahr	–
Bürgerliches Brauhaus G.m.b.H.; Keetmanshooper Brauerei und Mineralwasser Fabrik Karl Fischer & Co	Keetmanshooop	Founded in 1911, now closed	Karl Fischer	–

Karibiber Brauerei und Mineralwasserfabrik	Karibib	Active around 1912, now closed	C. Hanke	–
Kronenbrauerei	Swakopmund	Founded in 1912, now closed	Johann Heuschneider	Kronenbrau
Felsenkellerbrauerei Omaruru	Omaruru	Founded in 1917, now closed	Conrad Piehl	Omaruru Urquell
Kronenbrauerei	Windhoek	Founded in 1919, now closed	Johann Heuschneider	Kronenbrau
South West Breweries/Namibia Breweries	Windhoek	Founded in 1920	Carl List, E. Behnsen, Werner List, Bernd Masche, Sven Thieme	Windhoek Pilsner, Windhoek Löwen Bräu, Windhoek Extra Stout, Spring Bock, Tafel Lager, Windhoek Lager, Windhoek Light, Windhoek Export, Windhoek Special, Urbock, Maibock, Camelthorn Weissbier, King Lager
Union Brewery	Windhoek	1922–1928	Johann Heuschneider, Ludwig Barella	–
Hansa Brewery	Swakopmund	1928–2005	Johann Heuschneider	Tafel Lager, Urbock
Tunweni Brewery	Tsumeb	Founded 1997, now closed	Part of NBL	–
Camelthorn Brewery	Windhoek	2008–2012	Jörg Finkeldei	Weizen, American Red Ale, Helles, Gold, Fresh, Bok beer, Sundowner

Swakopmund Brewing Company	Swakopmund	Founded in 2015	–	Three changing beers
Welwitschia Brewery/SABMiller Namibia	Okahandja	Founded in 2014	–	Carling Black Label, Castle Lager, Castle Lite
Skeleton Coast Brewery	Hentiesbay	Founded in 2015	Stiaan Cloete	The Dunedin Star, The Captain's Courage
Namib Dunes Craft Brewery	Swakopmund	Founded in 2016	Du Preez Calitz, André Genis	IPA, Belgian Witbier, Blonde, Weiss, and Irish Red

Appendix 2: Traditional Brewing Recipes

As already mentioned in the prelude of this book, beer has been produced in Namibia for centuries. Even after the introduction of modern brewing facilities, people kept producing so-called 'traditional' beer to this day. The recipes noted down below illustrate the inventiveness of humankind, using the materials that are available while adapting to the challenging climates of Namibia. A variety of beers are made from beans, potatoes, honey and other ingredients, using trees, the earth and other elements of nature to ferment the drink. Today, drinks such as *tombo* are well known around the country. However, other drinks are largely forgotten, and their recipes are (almost) lost. During the archival research of this project, several of these old recipes were found by accident, for instance in colonial reports from German or South African governments. A selection is published below, to give an idea of how these drinks were made. The original description of each recipe is quoted, including the colonial terms that were used at the time.

Kaffir-beer[1]

The following are the ingredients used in the preparation of this decoction — all, any one or a combination being used — they are raw potatoes, potato peels, peas or split peas, beans, mealies, raisins and certain starchy roots, and for fermentation sugar and Florylin[2] are usually used, or otherwise golden syrup and any other yeast that is procurable. The method of preparation varies somewhat but the general principle is the same.

The usual manner in which this drink is made is as follows:

About one gallon of water is placed in a suitable receptacle (barrel, paraffin, tin, etc.) and heated, but not to boiling point. To this is added 4 lbs sugar and the contents stirred until the sugar has been completely dissolved. Then a few pounds of peas (usually split peas) and about ten unpealed [sic] potatoes which have previously been cut into small pieces are added. Cold water is then added until the receptacle is almost filled with lukewarm water. To hasten fermentation yeast may then also be added. This mixture is made to ferment by keeping the receptacle warm with skins and blankets or by burying it in the earth

---

[1] NAN, F002-RARA/062, Native beverages 1931.
[2] Florylin is the German brand name of a low-activity form of active-dried yeast and was used before the 1900s. Although it is unlikely that the local population in (German) South West Africa used this particular brand, it is possible that they used a similar form of yeast. Presumably the colonial officer who wrote this account interpreted this kind of yeast as Florylin, which was used in Germany. See: A.H. Rose and J.S. Harrison (eds.), *The Yeasts: Yeast Technology* (London 1993) 366.

so as to escape detection. It is left until it has lost the taste of sugar. The fermentation is allowed to proceed for 24 hours or even two or three days. According to the duration of fermentation the mixture contains a larger or smaller amount of alcohol. When ready for use it is strained and the strained liquid is the kaffir-beer. The residue is frequently used again, the only addition being sugar and water. The brewing is usually done by womenfolk and some have a better reputation for brewing beer than others. In fact there are "professional" brewers. The percentage of alcohol varies but a potency of at least 6% alcohol is usually obtained. It is stated that to give the drink a "bite" tobacco is added as an ingredient and it is also not uncommon for methylated spirits to be added to the finished product. This gives some idea of the vicious concoctions that are sometimes drunk.

Honey-beer[3]

Honey is mixed with the crushed bark of the Omuama tree or the crushed root of the bitter Ojiti tree in a receptacle of lukewarm water. The receptacle is carefully covered up and the mixture is left fermenting for 12 to 24 hours. This beer was excellently brewed by the Nama and their subjects, the Bergdama.

Sugar-beer[4]

In a suitable receptacle (barrel, paraffin tin, etc.) 4-10 lbs. of sugar are mixed with a few pounds of peas and about ten potatoes cut into small bits in hot water. Cold water is then added until the receptacle is filled with lukewarm water. This mixture is made to ferment by keeping the receptacle warm with skins and blankets or by burying it in the earth to escape detection, until it has lost its taste of sugar. This beer is brewed by the Hereros, Namas, Bergdama and Bastards. Small differences are attained by adding other substances, e.g. mealie-meal, boer-meal, beans, etc.

Marewu (pronounced Michau)[5]

Marewu is a beverage prepared from mealie meal and water to which a little flour is added. It is quite a wholesome drink provided these ingredients are adhered to, but by the addition of sugar and yeast an intoxicating beverage can be obtained – probably the purest made. The longer fermentation is allowed to proceed the more potent the drink becomes. The intoxicating beverage is prepared by cooking mealie meal to a very fine consistence.

---

[3] H. Vedder, 'Notes on the Brewing of Kaffir Beer in S.W.A.: A History of Beer', *Journal of the South West Africa Scientific Society*, Vol. 3 (1951) 41–43.
[4] Ibid.
[5] NAN, F002-RARA/062, Native beverages 1931.

It is then allowed to cool and a little flour is added. A quantity of water is then added and the mixture allowed to stand overnight when it is ready for use. The supernatant fluid and the residue are both partaken of.

Omaongo[6]

The fully ripe marula fruits are allowed to drop to the ground, upon which they are gathered and stored in heaps. Once there are enough, the women and girls press the juice out of them. Each one holds a pointed horn in her right hand, while two containers are positioned in front of her. She takes a fruit with her left hand, pierces it with the horn, loosening the kernel. The juice is left to ferment for 12 days. Water is poured over the kernels, to which some flesh is usually still attached, and this, too, is left to ferment, producing a significantly weaker omaongo which is usually drunk by women and children and called *oshinway*.

---

[6] NAN, F002-NAMZ 0559, J. Silvester, A trail of broken beer bottles, the Namibian Weekender, 10/09/99.

www.ingramcontent.com/pod-product-compliance
Lightning Source LLC
Chambersburg PA
CBHW080808300426
44114CB00020B/2865